PROMISES BETRAYED

AN AFGHAN INTERPRETER AT THE FALL OF KABUL

PROMISES BETRAYED

AN AFGHAN INTERPRETER AT THE FALL OF KABUL

JAMIL HASSAN

FOREWORD BY
GENERAL DAVID PETRAEUS

ABOOKS

Alive Book Publishing

Additional copies may be ordered from the publisher for
educational, business, promotional or premium use.
For information, contact ALIVE Book Publishing at:
alivebookpublishing.com

Book Interior and Cover Design by Alex P. Johnson

Cover Photo by Air Force Senior Airman Taylor Crul
About the Cover: *Airmen load qualified evacuees aboard a C-17
Globemaster III aircraft at Hamid Karzai International Airport,
Kabul, Afghanistan, Aug. 21, 2021.*

ISBN 13
978-1-63132-168-9 Deluxe Color Hardback
978-1-63132-169-6 Deluxe Color Paperback
978-1-63132-171-9 Standard Paperback
978-1-63132-170-2 Ebook

Library of Congress Control Number: 2022943013
Library of Congress Cataloging-in-Publication Data
is available upon request.

First Edition

Published in the United States of America by ALIVE Book Publishing
an imprint of Advanced Publishing LLC, Alamo, California, USA
alivebookpublishing.com

PRINTED IN THE UNITED STATES OF AMERICA

10 9 8 7 6 5 4 3 2 1

DEDICATION

I dedicate this book to my wife who stood strong with me during the evacuation; to my young daughter who suffered a lot along the journey not knowing what was going on; to my people who have lost their twenty years of achievements; to my fellow Afghans who have escaped the Taliban only to begin new lives from scratch in other countries around the world.

And last but not least, I dedicate this book to all the Afghans who served alongside the foreign forces in Afghanistan but were left behind by the US and its allies.

I hope this book will draw the world's attention back to Afghanistan, so that its people may enjoy living in peace and prosperity, once again.

My great concern is not whether you have failed,
but whether you are content with your failure.

—Abraham Lincoln

ACKNOWLEDGMENTS

Along the evacuation journey, I met a lot of wonderful people. They wanted to know about the chaotic withdrawal of all foreign forces from Afghanistan and what followed. They patiently listened when I told them about what thousands of other Afghans and I had been through. I am grateful, from the bottom of my heart, to all those who helped me, directly or indirectly, write this book. One of them was Mrs. Lorie Aisha Shinwari, a U.S. citizen whom I met during the final leg of my evacuation journey at U.S. Army Base Fort McCoy, Wisconsin. She encouraged me to write a book about my story because, according to her, it was worth sharing with others as it would give them a clearer picture of what had happened on August 15, 2021 and beyond. Secondly, I extend my gratitude to Eric Johnson, the COO at Alive Book Publishing, and his entire team. For over the past six months, Eric was so deeply involved in this project that I sometimes thought it was *his* own book, not mine. I also admire Steve Wagner, Alive's editor and writing coach. Steve's work gave a totally different perspective to the book, taking it from a personal story of the mismanaged evacuation to a comprehensive and chronicled analysis of the twenty years of the so-called, "War on Terror." Most important of all, there are no words with which to adequately *thank* US Army General David Petraeus, who reviewed the entire text of the book before it was published.

CONTENTS

FOREWORD

During the many years that I was privileged to command US and Coalition Forces in Iraq, Afghanistan, and the greater Middle East, our forces were critically enabled by host nation battlefield interpreters—'terps,' for short. Terps didn't just translate during the interactions of our men and women on the ground with local leaders and citizens, they also provided indispensable insights on the most important element in those wars—the population or, as we often described it, the 'human terrain.' In performing their vital function, Terps shared risk and hardship with our forces on the ground, provided invaluable service to them, and, on a number of occasions, even saved the lives of the coalition force members with whom they were working.

Tragically, despite assurances to the contrary and the Special Immigrant Visa created for terps and their families in 2008, the United States left behind many tens of thousands of terps and their family members during our chaotic departure from Afghanistan in August 2021. Recent estimates put the number of terps and family members still in Afghanistan at as many as 160,000.

The security of those we left behind is seriously jeopardized by their work with our forces; in fact, well over 1,000 terps have been killed over the years while waiting to receive final approval of a Special Immigrant Visa. And large numbers of them live in fear today, as the Taliban regime, which they helped us fight, targets them and their family members.

Promises Betrayed is the extraordinary story of Jamil Hassan, one of the Afghan interpreters who managed to escape and make his way to America. His first-hand account of his and his family's experiences is absolutely riveting. It is also illuminating, full of insights, and inspirational — while inevitably prompting, as well, reflections that include anguish, frustration, and anger, as Jamil's story reminds us of important work that is very much unfinished.

This, then, is the compelling story of one of our many extraordinary Afghan terps in the War in Afghanistan—one who proved to be particularly determined, resourceful, and intrepid.

To understand our engagement in Afghanistan, America's longest war, one has to understand the role of the courageous Afghan terps, many of whom served multiple "tours" alongside our men and women on the ground against a tenacious enemy in the most challenging of environments and contexts imaginable. *Promises Betrayed* provides that understanding.

Given all that, I encourage you to read this important book and also to recommend it to others—and then to join the voices calling on our government to meet the unfulfilled moral obligation we still have to those who served on the ground with our forces but are left behind in the shadow of the Hindu Kush.

—*General David Petraeus, US Army (Ret.), former Commander of the Surge in Iraq, US Central Command, and NATO/US Forces in Afghanistan, and former Director of the CIA*

Note From The Publisher

On January 15, 2022, I received a notification through our website chat service that Mr. Abdul Jamil Hassan wanted to speak with someone in our office about publishing a book.

He had written about his experience as an Afghan refugee — one of the "lucky ones" — who had managed to escape with his wife and young daughter from the Hamid Karzai International airport in Kabul during the calamitous evacuation just five months prior, on August 18, 2021. I connected with Jamil by email, and four days later, on Wednesday, January 19th , we met in my Alamo, California office.

After hearing Mr. Hassan's compelling eyewitness account, I knew his story had to be shared with the world. People everywhere — Americans in particular — needed to know the full, inside story, from an Afghan ally's perspective, about our botched withdrawal from Kabul.

As someone who has worked in media for two decades, I knew that my perspective on our involvement in Afghanistan was much like it was for many Americans — shaped primarily by politically-motivated, Western-biased narratives. We know the "truth" about Afghanistan, only by what has been reported to us through various filters. The information we receive, and the stories we are told, vary, depending upon who's telling the story, and why.

While every refugee's story matters, Mr. Hassan's is important because he served as a high-level interpreter and translator for coalition forces, having worked for both the American and Italian military. Because he was fluent in both of the languages spoken in Afghanistan—Pashto and Dari—much of his service was with senior coalition officers.

Hassan had served as a translator for General David Petraeus in one high-level meeting and worked in a regular capacity for General John Nicholson, who was the longest-serving commander of U.S. and NATO forces in Afghanistan. This meant that Jamil Hassan and his family were, and are now, high-value targets for possible Taliban retribution. They *had* to leave Afghanistan immediately; their security—indeed their very lives—were in mortal danger if they stayed.

So, on August 15, 2021, as events unfolded in Kabul making it clear that Taliban would soon be in control of the entire country, Jamil scrambled to get himself and his family to the airport, hoping for evacuation.

In the pages that follow you'll read Jamil's minute-by-minute and day-by-day account of that experience, as he and his family, by the narrowest of margins, eventually made their way onto a plane and out of Kabul. Their journey took them to Qatar, Germany, Virginia, and finally to California, where they now live in the San Francisco East Bay Area.

But the story does not end here.

Over the past several months, because Jamil is still in touch with family and friends now trapped in Afghanistan, we have become aware of increasingly severe, negative repercussions of the botched withdrawal. And this, dear reader, brings me to the reason why reading—and understanding—this story is so critically important.

First, it is important to know Mr. Hassan's motivations in writing his story. As the war in Ukraine has taken center stage in the media, he, and we at ALIVE Books, fear that the public is already forgetting about the tragedy that occurred in August 2021, and we want to make Americans aware that things are growing worse every day for those left behind in Afghanistan. Also, Mr. Hassan's hope for any commercial success from this book's publication is primarily focused on helping his fellow Afghans who are still trapped behind enemy lines, as proceeds from its sale will be directed toward helping continued evacuation efforts.

Second, it is also important to know that even though Mr. Hassan and his immediate family are now safe here in America, and while they are grateful to be here, the price they paid for serving alongside us is greater than you might imagine.

Like many Afghans, Jamil Hassan believed in what our leaders were selling—the hope for a better life and a better future. He served alongside our troops and worked toward personal goals that were all anchored on promises made by *our* country—and by extension, by you and me.

In August 2021, those promises were broken. Everything Jamil Hassan—along with countless American and coalition soldiers—worked for, was swept aside during those disastrous weeks in August. For all intents and purposes his home country is lost—probably forever. The fate of Jamil's friends and family members left behind is tenuous at best, and anything of substance that Jamil Hassan had built for his family and his country was all washed away by the disastrous decisions and actions made by President Joe Biden.

It is sobering to realize how fortunate we are as Americans. We have never experienced anything even close to what our Afghan allies experienced and are now experiencing. Here in America, we tend to forget each world tragedy, moving on to the next one as though it is all just another form of entertainment.

But this story was not written to entertain you. It was written and published in the hope that you would put yourself in Jamil Hassan's shoes; that you would know the feeling of having no choice but to leave family, friends, loved ones, and the life you had built, behind.

Remarkably, Mr. Hassan is not bitter. He is thankful that he and his family were evacuated, and while they arrived here with little more than the clothes they were wearing, he is looking forward to rebuilding their lives here in the USA.

And as you think about this, my plea to you is that you also think about how we got here. The broader implications might best be framed in President Obama's words: "Elections have consequences."

As a nation made up of freedom-loving people, we—you and me—must hold our leaders to account. We elect them to serve us; to speak for us, especially in matters of global consequence.

I expect them to keep their word because their word is my word. It is your word. It is America's word.

Author's Preface

I have been very active on Facebook since I was a student at Kabul University. I posted just about everything, from supporting the Afghan government and forces, to criticizing the Taliban, to posting photos of my wedding and visits with friends, to sharing my achievements and promoting those of others. After the evacuation of my family and thousands of other Afghans in mid-2021, I considered writing about it on Facebook to let people know that it wasn't a comfortable journey for those fleeing the country. But, as the process became more prolonged, I concluded that I couldn't tell this story only in Facebook posts. I chose to wait and instead share my story with others once I was settled in the U.S.

It took my family—me, my wife, and our young daughter—more than two-and-a-half months to get from Kabul to California. Along the way, I met many nice people, and some encouraged me to write an article about my story. But every time I attempted to do that, I realized that the story was simply too broad to fit into a short narrative. It would have to be a full-fledged book.

After I finished writing the manuscript, I was faced with the daunting task of somehow publishing my story. I was new to the U.S. and had no idea what steps to take or even who I should approach. I reached out to two friends who had been studying in the States for several years and told them I was writing a book about what had happened in

Afghanistan, and how my family and I had been evacuated. I asked them if it was possible to have their professors take a look at it and advise me about what my next steps should be.

Then, on the morning of January 15, 2022, I was searching for something on the internet, and it suddenly occurred to me to search for publishing firms. After sending an email to one of them, I noticed that the Alive Book Publishing website offered a live chat option. I started chatting with a lady named Kristi, and after the initial greetings, I wrote, "I am an Afghan refugee who worked with U.S. forces as an interpreter. My family and I were recently evacuated from Afghanistan to Northern California. I have written a memoir about the experience and hope to publish it."

She was very nice to me, and towards the end of our conversation, she wrote, "On a personal note, I am so sorry that our current administration was not better prepared, and that they allowed the losses in your home country. Most Americans feel that we let you and your country down."

These two sentences established a strong connection and I felt deep in my heart that I had found the right publisher for this book. I even asked Kristi to email me the transcript of our conversation so I could preserve what felt like the first truly hopeful thing that had happened to me in the U.S.

Within days of that first conversation, I met with Eric Johnson at Alive Book Publishing. He has been supportive and generous from the beginning, and it was because of his advice that I decided to include pictures in the book, to help readers identify with me and my story. He later introduced me to Steve Wagner, who became my editor and writing coach. Steve did an incredible job of keeping the story true to my original intent and communicated with me directly throughout the process to ensure accuracy and clarity.

What is more important is that Steve's advice helped me add an inclusive analysis of what has been happening in my home country over the past four decades. None of this would have happened if Kristi hadn't chatted with me that day. Though I might have found another publisher, the fact that Alive Book Publishing was just a fifteen-minute drive from where I lived made things so much easier. I met with Eric and his team in person nearly every week for several months to discuss relevant matters.

I hope my story will inspire you and bring perspective and empathy to the plight of the Afghan people, because this isn't just a personal account of what my family and I went through during our evacuation and immigration. There were more than one hundred thousand of my fellow Afghans evacuated from Kabul who faced similar or even more terrifying ordeals than we did. Therefore, it's *their* story, too.

This book is also an assessment of America's diminishing image as the leader of the free world because of the failure in Afghanistan, coupled with Russia's invasion of Ukraine. The American people need to know that the number of countries that are questioning their country's resolve and competence is rising. The world is now doubting whether or not the U.S. can be relied upon as a responsible partner on the world stage.

The main purpose of this book, however, is to shift the world's attention back towards the ongoing crisis in Afghanistan. It is imperative that it does not again become a safe haven for international terrorist groups like Al-Qaeda and ISIS (Islamic State of Iraq and Syria). I also implore the U.S. and EU countries to address the condition of thousands of Afghan refugees who still face an uncertain future.

In addition, I have decided to donate a portion of the money that I realize from this book to help Afghan immigrants get resettled. Hopefully, it will help them to pay their rent, furnish their homes, buy clothes for their children, or anything else they might need. I will also donate a portion of the proceeds to charities in Afghanistan to help those in desperate need back home, as it has been estimated that more than 95 percent of Afghans now live under the poverty line.

Additionally, it is worth noting that a number of my family members are still in Afghanistan. The Taliban have searched my house twice in Kabul and threatened them. I have wrestled with the fact that my family in Afghanistan might come under increasing suspicion because of this book, but I feel that there is a greater good to be served by my story. I am committed to bringing the attention of the world to the plight of my thirty million fellow Afghans. It is already late, but if the world doesn't act quickly, it will be *too* late.

INTRODUCTION

The terrorist attacks in New York and Washington D.C. on September 11, 2001, in which nearly three thousand people from ninety-three countries perished, were the deadliest assaults on U.S. soil since Japan attacked Pearl Harbor in 1941. Then-U.S. President George W. Bush accused Al-Qaeda and its leader, Osama Bin Laden, of carrying out the attacks. He was believed to be hiding in Afghanistan, which by then had been under Taliban control for over five years. After they refused to turn him over to the U.S., American and British military planes began bombing Al-Qaeda and Taliban forces in Afghanistan on October 7, 2001. Though the Taliban were removed from power and Al-Qaeda was seriously crippled, allied forces continued to confront a stubborn Taliban insurgency, while also rebuilding the infrastructure in Afghanistan and establishing what would later become the Afghan National Defense and Security Forces (ANDSF). The American and British troops were later joined by forty-three NATO member and partner countries after the United Nations authorized the International Security Assistance Force (ISAF) on December 20, 2001. At its peak, there were an estimated 130,000 foreign troops in Afghanistan.

A decade into the war, in November 2010 at a summit in Lisbon (Portugal), NATO member countries signed a declaration agreeing to hand over full responsibility for security to the ANDSF by the end of 2014. Following that, on June 22, 2011, then-U.S. President Barak Obama announced the drawdown of American forces in Afghanistan. It is believed that NATO's Lisbon declaration of 2010, coupled with Obama's 2011 announcement, were the main reasons that the Taliban realized that they *could* defeat the U.S. and its allies, including the ANDSF, if they simply waited out the foreign troops and choose an advantageous time to act.

Less than a year later, in January 2012, the U.S. struck a deal with the Taliban allowing the group to open a "political office" in Doha, Qatar. This implicitly indicated that America no longer considered the Taliban to be a terrorist group since the U.S. maintained a strict policy of refusal to negotiate with terrorists. On the other hand, it was a significant achievement for the Taliban and signaled the eventual demise of the West-backed government in Afghanistan. The move was reminiscent of the mujahideen's political stance in the late 1980s in Pakistan, which finally toppled the Soviet-backed government of President Najibullah in 1991. Additionally, the Doha office provided freedom of movement to Taliban leaders who embarked on frequent trips to Russia, China, and Iran (all archrivals of the U.S.), among other destinations. The U.S., however, received relatively nothing in exchange for this loosening of restrictions.

Finally, on December 28, 2014, the U.S. and NATO ended their combat missions in Afghanistan and the ANDSF officially took the lead in all operations. This was a major step towards victory for the Taliban as it essentially opened the door for them to increase attacks on the ANDSF on the battlegrounds. And when the U.S. signed a deal with the Taliban in Doha on February 29, 2020, Taliban fighters carried out dozens of attacks on the ANDSF as the deal didn't call for an immediate cease-fire in the days after its signing. Even worse, the U.S.-Taliban deal had two classified annexes about which no Afghan, and allegedly not even Afghan President Ashraf Ghani, had any knowledge.

One of the conditions of the Doha agreement was that the U.S. would work on a plan for the release of the Taliban's combat and political prisoners. The officially titled "Agreement for Bringing Peace to Afghanistan between the Islamic Emirate of Afghanistan which is not recognized by the United States as a state and is known as the Taliban and the United States of America," explicitly states that this was "a confidence-building measure with the coordination and approval of all relevant sides." It further decrees that "up to five thousand prisoners of the Islamic Emirate of Afghanistan (which is not recognized by the United States as a state and are known as the Taliban), and up to one thousand prisoners of the other side (the Afghan government) will be released by March 10, 2020."

The prisoner exchange was completed in early September 2020, and a large percentage of the Taliban prisoners returned to the battlefield. Again, the Taliban made significant achievements while the U.S. didn't receive much in return. Eventually, by announcing the full withdrawal of all American troops from Afghanistan, President Biden hammered the final nail into the coffin of a burgeoning but persistent democracy in Afghanistan.

Initially, the U.S. and its allies fought quite successfully alongside the ANDSF for years, but things took a serious turn for the worse when America stopped fighting the joint enemy and instead began negotiations with the Taliban. By the middle of 2021, it was widely suspected that the U.S. would soon hand Afghanistan back to the Taliban on a proverbial silver platter. Therefore, sacrificing one's life for the sake of his/her country meant nothing for most ANDSF members, which is why Afghan soldiers did not resist Taliban militants. Cities and provinces were soon falling like dominoes to the repressive theocratic group.

With regard to the calculation of the cost of the war, the number of U.S. military personnel and U.S. Department of Defense (DOD) civilians killed in Afghanistan from October 7, 2001 (when the war began) to December 31, 2014 (when the combat mission ended), stands at around 2,200, while those killed between January 2015 and September 2021 number approximately 110, including the 13 U.S. Marines killed in a suicide bomb explosion at a Kabul Airport gate during the August 2021 evacuation. These developments indicate that when primarily supporting the ANDSF (beyond 2014), the U.S. significantly reduced its casualties in Afghanistan, while the number of ANDSF deaths skyrocketed right after they took full responsibility for security in the country. The same rubric also applies to the military expenditures incurred by the U.S. and its allies.

The financial cost of the war is well over $1 trillion, while the death toll stands at 3,600-plus foreign troops, 4,000-plus foreign contractors, 70,000-plus ANDSF, 50,000-plus Taliban and other militant groups, 50,000-plus Afghan civilians, 444-plus aid workers, and 72 journalists. Moreover, two million Afghans became refugees in Iran and Pakistan in the beginning of 2021, with more than six hundred thousand others internally displaced. And over one hundred thousand Afghans, most of them highly educated, were evacuated by the U.S. and its allies to America and Europe after the Taliban took Kabul on August 15, 2021.

More importantly, this time, the Taliban have returned to power with more militants and are controlling more territory than they did in the late 1990s and Al-Qaeda has been replaced by ISIS. The return of the Taliban to power, ongoing violations of human rights by the group, a widespread famine, and the influx of refugees into Iran and Pakistan have so far been the noticeable consequences of President Biden's decision to leave Afghanistan once and for all.

Now, the U.S. and its allies must deal with the aftermath of the withdrawal, the costs of which have already exceeded hundreds of millions of dollars, while thousands of America's Afghan allies still remain in Afghanistan, and in refugee camps in Pakistan, Qatar, the United Arab Emirates (UAE), some EU countries and elsewhere, waiting for relocation to the U.S. Poverty and hunger are once again an everyday reality for the Afghan people. It is entirely reasonable to suggest that the sacrifices of thousands of American, NATO and ANDSF troops, as well as Afghan civilians killed in the conflict, plus the billions of dollars of U.S. taxpayers' money invested in Afghanistan over the course of twenty years, became moot on August 15, 2021. On that fateful day, twenty years of extremely hard-fought gains were erased.

CHAPTER ONE
THE COLLAPSE OF KABUL

*Taliban militants inside the Afghan presidential palace in
Kabul, August 15, 2021. Photo by Zabi Karimi, AP*

I received the news that would change my life on the
morning of August 15, 2021. I was busy supervising the
painting of a room in preparation for my younger
brother's wedding two weeks hence in Kabul, the capital of
Afghanistan, when the phone rang. On the line was my
wife's brother, Haseebullah Talash, who worked as the senior digital editor for the Afghanistan branch of Radio Free
Europe/Radio Liberty. He had just left the Passport General
Directorate, the main entity for issuing passports in the
country. His voiced was rattled.

"I have been running for over an hour. The Taliban are
here. They are about to enter the city. Do not leave the house.

If you are outside, get home as soon as possible," he said in Pashto, one of the two official languages of Afghanistan (Dari being the other). I was shocked and wondered how this could be possible. As I understood it, there were tens of thousands of American forces and ANDSF in Kabul to keep precisely such a takeover from happening.

I lived on the fourth floor of a building in the Russian-named Mackroryan, a complex of multistory concrete buildings constructed by the Soviets between 1950s-1970s. I wasn't far from the U.S. Embassy and the headquarters of NATO's Resolute Support Mission (RSM). While talking on the phone on the balcony of my apartment, I saw black smoke hovering over the U.S. Embassy. I could only assume that they were burning sensitive documents and materials.

I ran back inside and turned on the TV to see both local and global channels showing footage of people running wildly in every direction, while others were trapped in cars as chaos unfolded in the streets of Kabul. As my brother-in-law described the Taliban coup, he recalled a chilling detail: "I saw Afghan policemen quickly changing from their uniforms to ordinary Afghan clothes and escaping even before the civilians could leave."

As late as three o'clock that day, Afghan President Ashraf Ghani and his defense and interior ministers were still trying to convince the people that Kabul would not fall to the Taliban, and that even if it did happen, there wouldn't be bloodshed. In what turned out to be his last statement from Arg, the presidential palace, President Ghani said:

"It is an obvious necessity, so I have instructed the Ministries of Defense and Interior Affairs to have forces from the National Directorate of Security along with the National Police and the National Army take full responsibility for the security of all residents. It is our responsibility, and it is a responsibility that, God willing, we will take on appropriately. Secondly, those people that are thinking of rioting, looting, and killing people will be dealt with in full force. My request is to establish phone lines for complaints and information directly to both the Interior and Defense Ministries, and especially to the National Directorate of Security so that the networks of people including neighborhood representatives, police districts, and local councils are contactable."

An hour later, news broke that Ghani and all other high-ranking Afghan government officials had fled the country.

While the crisis was intensifying throughout the day, an increasing number of U.S. and NATO Chinook helicopters could be seen flying over Kabul. I soon learned that most of the Western embassies, including that of the U.S., had relocated to Kabul International Airport (also known as HKIA— Hamid Karzai International Airport, name after Ghani's predecessor). Meanwhile, prisoners from the notorious Pul-e-Charkhi Prison, the largest jail in Afghanistan located in the east of Kabul city, had broken loose. Among them were hundreds of Taliban, Al-Qaeda, and ISIS-K (the ISIS branch mostly active in eastern Afghanistan) militants, as well as other criminals. Thousands of Taliban as well as Al-Qaeda and other militants had been captured and imprisoned by the ANDSF since 2002. The Taliban always released prisoners when they captured a province, which of course added to their manpower and ability to intimidate their enemies. In one of the videos that I saw posted on Facebook, three prisoners who were still inside Pul-e-Charkhi had filmed themselves, declaring, "We are free! We are coming for you!" as they threatened those they blamed for their incarceration.

Initially, the Taliban announced that they would not enter the city without coordination with the Kabul administration, a term they used throughout the American occupation to refer to the U.S.-backed government of Afghanistan. But Taliban forces quickly overran Kabul. Videos of them entering different parts of the city and occupying police districts (the equivalent of police stations/departments in the U.S.) soon made the rounds on social media. In most of them, Taliban militants and commanders claimed that they had entered Kabul only to prevent the looting of public and private properties. And in nearly all of the videos, entire districts looked to be abandoned by the police, so the Taliban faced no resistance. At nine o'clock on that first night, the Taliban decreed a strict curfew that I heard via the loudspeakers from a mosque near my house:

"No one shall leave their homes between 9:00 p.m. and 8:00 a.m. so that the mujahideen of the Islamic Emirate of Afghanistan can identify those who intend to loot public and private properties, and to prevent them from doing so."

As Kabul fell, the Association of Wartime Allies (AWA) Advocacy Group warned that the Taliban would conduct door-to-door searches and strongly advised everyone to destroy anything that documented their work with foreigners. The AWA Advocacy Group was a Facebook page established by members of the U.S. Congress, the U.S. military, and Afghan interpreters to help SIV applicants with their cases. SIV stands for Special Immigration Visa and is a U.S. Department of State program established to help Afghans and Iraqis who worked for the U.S. military as interpreters to immigrate to the U.S., thereby escaping Taliban reprisal for conspiring with enemy forces. As I followed the news on social media, I realized that most pro-government people who worked for the Afghan government or for Western countries and organizations had already removed their profile pictures, and some had even deactivated their accounts. They all knew that the Taliban would be seeking reprisals from anyone who had worked with foreign forces.

This stark and undeniable fact presented me with a serious problem. I had worked as an interpreter for foreign military troops (specifically, Italians and Americans) from 2008 to 2012, and then again from 2017 to 2021. I had dozens of letters of recommendation, letters of appreciation, and certificates and coins awarded by high-ranking Italian and American military officers. I had two letters of appreciation from U.S. Army General (Four-Star) John W. Nicholson, and a coin from U.S. Army General (Four-Star) David McNeill, both commanders of U.S. and NATO forces in Afghanistan. Also, I had hundreds of pictures from the eight years I had worked for U.S. and Italian troops, including a picture with then-commander of CENTCOM, U.S. Army General (Four-Star) David Petraeus. I had copies of all my contracts, letters of employment, and job descriptions. And most valuable in terms of my immediate future, I had fifty-plus pages of documents for my SIV case. My interview at the U.S. Embassy in Kabul was scheduled for August 30, 2021, for which I had prepared a complete package including passport-size photos that were required for visas for myself, my wife, and our infant daughter.

Worse than that, it was impossible for me to delete all the posts I had made over the previous ten years on Facebook speaking out against the Taliban or in support of the Afghan government, and I couldn't deactivate my account because I had to follow the AWA Advocacy Group. I knew that the group would be a crucial ally in the coming days, and that

I would need access to their information and support if I were to move my family to safety. I decided to keep my Facebook account and simply delete as many posts as possible. I also removed my profile picture and cover photo, and removed the photo from my WhatsApp account.

For many years, as foreign forces were focused on winning the hearts and minds of the Afghan people, the Taliban concluded that in order to thwart their missions, they needed to target the interpreters. If there were no interpreters, the foreign forces could not communicate with the local population and, in times of joint operations, with the ANDSF. Initially, interpreters were easily identified as they did not wear military uniforms. Once the Taliban's course of action was discovered, foreign forces began issuing uniforms to the interpreters. Still, they were easily identified because they did not carry weapons. To counter this, foreign forces placed interpreters among their troops on foot patrols.

When the U.S. initially began the relocation of Afghan interpreters several months before the fall of Kabul, the Taliban were well aware of the plan and quickly tracked down people they considered "spies of the infidels." If the Taliban captured travelling members of the ANDSF, they would demand guarantees that they would not serve in the ranks of ANDSF any longer. But when they captured interpreters, the Taliban had orders to execute them on the spot.

One of the tactics that the Taliban used to identify ANDSF members and interpreters was by establishing checkpoints on roads and stopping any vehicle they deemed suspicious. They would ask anyone who looked frightened for their phone. Then, they would dial a random number on the phone, telling the person on the other end that they were members of the ANDSF and that they had detained an individual for working with the Taliban. If the person on the other end said that the detainee was an ANDSF member or an interpreter, they would face the Taliban's brutal punishment.

All of these factors created a reality wherein those who had worked with foreigners at any time saw no future for themselves and their children under the Taliban. And of course, many of us remembered the pre-2001 Taliban regime very well. We knew that women would be confined to their homes, girls would not be allowed to attend schools, men would be forced to grow beards and cut their hair short, watching television and listening to music would be banned, the economy would crash, there would be no employment, poverty and hunger would skyrocket, and no one would be allowed to criticize the regime. With all this in mind, most interpreters felt they had no choice but to evacuate and hopefully immigrate to a safe country, even though there would be significant danger in merely trying to leave Afghanistan.

I frantically sorted through all of my documents, took pictures of those for which I didn't have soft copies, and emailed them to my brothers, one in the U.S. and the other in Afghanistan. I also forwarded as many other emails as possible to them before deleting everything. Then, I tore all the documents and pictures into small pieces and asked my wife to burn them in the kitchen, bit-by-bit, so they would not produce any smoke. Then, I flushed the ashes down the toilet. I gave the coins to my younger brother to dispose of, to be scattered one by one into different dustbins around Mackroryan.

It took over ten hours to destroy or hide all the materials that would put me and my family in lethal danger from the Taliban who were looking to settle scores and establish an iron rule over Afghanistan. As an interpreter who had worked with occupying forces and the ANDSF, I would be firmly in their crosshairs if I were to be identified. In fact, if that were to occur, I was certain the Taliban would brand me as a collaborator with the "infidels" and execute me, and possibly my family, for what they would deem to be treasonous and heretical crimes.

CHAPTER TWO
LIFE UNDER THE TALIBAN

Taliban militants threatening a woman in Burqa, allegedly for leaving her house without a male guardian. (Reuters photo)

Afghanistan is a landlocked country located at the crossroads of South and Central Asia. It borders Pakistan to the east and south, Iran to the west, and three Central Asian countries (Tajikistan, Uzbekistan, and Turkmenistan) to the north. It also has a forty-six-mile, barely accessible border with China in the northeast. It has a population of over thirty-five million and its people are called Afghans. Its currency is *afghani*, a term that has been widely misused to refer to its citizens. Afghans come from more than twenty ethnic groups, with Pashtons, Tajiks, Hazaras, and Uzbeks making up the majority, respectively. Though the country's population is 99 percent Muslim,

Afghanistan's role in the connectivity between Asia and Europe through the ancient Silk Road has resulted in people of various linguistic and cultural backgrounds living in the country for centuries. The modern state's existence began in 1747 with the Durrani Empire, which spanned an area from eastern Iran to northern India. Later, Afghanistan became a buffer state between the British-ruled India and the Russian Empire. After three Anglo-Afghan wars, Afghanistan became an independent country in 1919. Known as the "Graveyard of Empires," due to its difficult terrain and long history of repelling foreign conquerors, Afghanistan has experienced and overcome multiple military incursions over the centuries, including those by Alexander the Great, Arab Muslims, the Mongols, the British, the Russians, and most recently the U.S.-led military coalition of over forty countries.

I wasn't yet born when the Union of Soviet Socialist Republics (U.S.S.R.), also known as the Soviet Union, deployed troops to Afghanistan on December 24, 1979, under the pretext of upholding the 1978 Soviet-Afghan Treaty of Friendship. They exiled the leader of the Parcham faction of the People's Democratic Party of Afghanistan (PDPA), and installed Babrak Karmal as the new head of the government. But even though the sitting President, Hafizullah Amin, was assassinated, the Afghan government did not collapse. The intervention was staged to ultimately establish a pro-Soviet government in Kabul. However, after a few years, Afghan resistance groups, called *Mujahideen*, started fighting the Soviets and Soviet-backed Afghan government forces across the country. The Afghan resistance soon became a proxy war for the West. Leaders of various Islamic political parties

16

of the Afghan mujahideen were welcomed in Pakistan where they were provided with funds, weapons, ammunition, offices, training, and direct financial support from Saudi Arabia and America's Operation Cyclone. This was America's largest covert operation ever (till then), which cost U.S. taxpayers around three billion dollars.

On November 12, 1987, Mohammad Yunus Khalis, the Chairman of the Union of Afghan mujahideen, was invited to Washington where he and his delegation, seeking to obtain more support from America, met with then-U.S. President Ronald Reagan. In the final years of the conflict, the U.S. provided Afghan mujahideen with Stingers—shoulder-launched anti-aircraft missiles. They proved very effective in bringing down Soviet and Afghan military aircraft, and eventually turned the tide of the war. At last, after a decade-long military presence and nearly fifteen thousand Soviet soldiers killed, the U.S.S.R. finally faced the inevitable and pulled its troops out of Afghanistan.

Following that, the country, and Kabul in particular, soon plunged into a devastating civil war. The Soviet-backed Afghan government of President Najibullah continued to fight the Afghan mujahideen for over three years but then, after he resigned and handed the government over to the U.S.-backed Afghan mujahideen, their various groups launched fierce battles against each other for control of Kabul. Each section of the city was controlled by a particular mujahideen group, and one needed to have written authorization to move from one side of the city to another.

The destruction caused by mujahideen infighting was even worse than that caused by the Soviets. The mujahideen had no knowledge about governance, and after they took possession of the Soviet military equipment and weapons from Afghan forces, they promptly deployed them against one another. The chaos and hardship the mujahideen brought upon Afghans gave birth to the Taliban movement which later provided room for Al-Qaeda to grow its ranks.

Meanwhile, convoys of Soviet food supplies were routinely ambushed, attacked, and looted by the mujahideen along the route to Kabul. At one point, people avoided eating fruit imported from Pakistan, suspecting it was being poisoned by the Pakistanis and Afghan mujahideen fighters in order to kill Afghan government officials who were the only ones that could afford the fruit. With this civil war, a real humanitarian crisis unfolded and soon people did not have access to potable water and basic foods.

As days passed, the fighting in Kabul intensified, and thousands never made it out of the city alive. More than half of the local population had already left for other provinces, but due to severe poverty, many could not survive there either. As a result, millions of Afghans migrated to Pakistan and Iran, leaving their belongings and homes behind. The mujahideen fighters searched civilians for cash and jewelry on their way out of Kabul. As people left, the city became a ghost town.

As far back as I can remember, my family and hundreds of others in our neighborhood lived in the crossfire of heavy artillery employed by two or more rival mujahideen factions. Civilians couldn't even make it to graveyards to bury loved ones killed in these battles—they buried them in their yards. During these years, people would spend months or even years in their basements, most of the time without any electricity. One couldn't find any part of the city that had not been ravaged by the conflict. Government buildings, schools, and hospitals were riddled with bullet holes or bombed into rubble. Our own apartment building was hit twice by Soviet tank rounds fired by the mujahideen. Once, the ammo and fuel depots at the Radio/Communication Battalion right across the street were hit, and they kept burning for over two days. That was the brightest and most illuminating light I remember seeing in my childhood years, a sad contrast to the countless days and nights I spent in our basement, hiding in the dark with my family.

I hail from Khuni Baghchah, a village in the Zurmat District of Afghanistan's eastern Paktia (pronounced as Paktya) province, about one hundred miles to the southeast of Kabul. The name of the village translates as "Garden of Bloodshed." It is said that it was originally called Khaani Baghcha, which means "Garden of the Rich." I was the third son born in my family. I have two older brothers, a sister, and a younger brother. My mother died from complications of Covid-19 in 2020. My father, now seventy-four and the oldest of his brothers, was the first one in his entire extended family who attended school.

Until before the U.S. invasion of Afghanistan in 2001, the general mentality in rural areas of Afghanistan had been that parents should not send their children to school because they would become kaffirs (infidels). The area where my father grew up was dominated by mullahs (religious clergy) and madrassas (religious schools). After he attended a few terms at one of the madrassas, my father's paternal uncle encouraged him to go to school. He was employed as an elementary school teacher immediately after finishing the ninth grade. When I was born in 1986, my father worked as an anchor for the state-run TV and radio station in Paktia.

At the time, Afghan mujahideen operated numerous offices, bases, and training centers in Paktia, which borders

Pakistan. It is believed that American and Saudi Arabian money was channeled to the mujahideen through the Pakistani army, particularly through its Inter-Services Intelligence (ISI). Less than half of the money made it to the Afghan mujahideen, while the rest was invested in Pakistan's armed forces and the development of its nuclear weapons program.

After the Soviets completed their retreat from Afghanistan in 1989, my family moved to Kabul. Three years later, the Soviet-backed government of President Najibullah collapsed and the mujahideen stormed the capital. Once during those days, a group of mujahideen came for one of our neighbors who was a high-ranking official in Najibullah's government and repossessed two cars that the government had provided for him. I still remember that one of the mujahideen militants handed me his binoculars so I could observe a military tank parked on a hilltop right across from our apartment building.

Many Afghans who are now living in America and Europe left the country before Najibullah's government toppled. Similarly, my father, fearing for his life, escaped to Iran. He stayed there for over a year while we—my mother, and at the time, four kids—were left on our own. We had no money, though thankfully my mother knew how to bake bread. Most women living in the Mackroryan used to work in the pre-mujahideen government and did not know how to bake bread. They provided the flour, and my mother did the baking. She received a few loaves of bread at the end of each day for her services, and this kept us from starving.

I was a kid and didn't really understand what was going on, but I still remember the days, weeks, and months we spent in the basements of the Mackroryan concrete buildings.

The only toys we played with were the cartridges of rounds. We found hundreds of them every morning. During the day, most people would remain on the stairs of their buildings because it shielded them from gunfire. One day, my mother was returning from the kitchen with some water when two Soviet tank rounds hit the wall behind her. Luckily, she wasn't injured, but our apartment was severely damaged. Since basically everyone in Kabul lived under a shared and constant threat, and it was the only world I had known, of course, I thought this was normal. Later, I came to understand that it wasn't normal at all.

After the mujahideen granted amnesty to former government employees, my father returned to Afghanistan, but by then, the scale of the civil war in Kabul was out of control. Instead of establishing an inclusive government, the various factions of the mujahideen were fighting each other on the streets of Kabul. After tolerating the conflicts for over a year, my family left Kabul for Jalalabad, the provincial capital of Nangarhar in eastern Afghanistan. Since Nangarhar borders Pakistan, Afghans who commuted to and from Pakistan needed to exchange Pakistani rupees for afghanis (the Afghan currency). My father started exchanging money at the bazaar while my two older brothers sold cigarettes and gum around Jalalabad. I enrolled at a government school and began attending classes in the morning and then selling cold water on the street in the afternoon.

One day, during my second year at school, my father said, "As soon as you are done with your classes, come to the bazaar. I will buy you some groceries."

Later that day, while I was at school playing with my classmates, suddenly there was a panic. Everyone came running out and I ran with them towards the city. Along the way, I peeled away from the group and started messing around, kicking sticks and stones while I walked. When I finally reached the downtown, I noticed that no one else was around. All the shops were closed and only a few Soviet-made military Jeeps and Toyota pickup trucks were moving around. There was a military tank in the middle of Talashi Square where I sold cold water every afternoon.

On the way back home, I saw a man in a military uniform lying on the ground in front of the provincial police headquarters, shot in the head. As I neared the alley leading to my home, I saw blood on the street and multiple bodies in front of shops. A crowd of people had gathered at the end of the alley and my father was among them. He was very angry and slapped me very hard before saying, "You fool, where were you?" Then he told me that the Taliban had taken over the government from the mujahideen.

Within days, the Taliban imposed strict Sharia rules. Among other impositions, they forced people to offer prayers at mosques, banned girls from going to school, asked all male students to wear black and/or white turbans, ordered every adult male to cut their hair and grow a beard, and instructed women not to leave home without a male guardian. Also, whenever they punished criminals, they forced people to gather around in particular areas to witness the punishments, which included whippings, amputations, and public executions by hanging or stoning to death.

The day the Taliban took control of Jalalabad was my sister's second day at school, and since they banned girls from attending school, she was very upset. Also, my father ordered that none of us go to school any longer as the Taliban would almost certainly change the school curriculums to reflect only their antiquated worldview.

My brothers kept on selling cigarettes and gum while I continued selling water on the side of a street. I had a wooden box, a bucket, and a plastic glass. I put the bucket over the box. One morning, as I was preparing to start the day, all of a sudden, the Taliban's chief of the traffic police for Jalalabad hit my box with his car, sending the bucket into the air. He instantly got off and slapped me on the face as hard as he could. He very clearly made his point; I must not block the street again. I got so angry, but could not do anything except pray for them to be removed from power as soon as possible. I promised myself that one day I would take my revenge in a much greater way if I had the power to do so.

We continued living under the Taliban rule in Jalalabad until one day, a man approached my father and demanded his identification. He eventually left but promised he would return soon. The following day, a friend of my father came and told him that some Taliban were on his tail, hoping to capture and punish him for his role in Najibullah's government. The next day, my family immigrated to Pakistan. My oldest brother and I immediately started working at a plastic shoe factory while my other brother found a job at a bakery. After two weeks, my father left Pakistan for Afghanistan's western Herat Province where he had a friend who had promised him safety and steady work without any fear of the Taliban. A year later, he returned, and my entire family went to Herat. It was an eight-day journey because the bus we were traveling in was very old and the highways were damaged, making it difficult for most vehicles to move faster than a crawl.

Nangarhar was less than a hundred miles east of Kabul. Even before the Taliban's rule, people in the province generally abided by the rules of Islam; women did not go out to the city often, and if they did, they were always accompanied by a male family member. Men kept their heads covered with white hats and only wore Afghan clothes, grew beards, and adhered to the strict practice of offering prayers five times a day at mosques. But the Taliban didn't just impose strict religious rituals and social restrictions, they also banned watching television, listening to music, and even flying kites. I still remember that once the Taliban saw a TV antenna in the area where my family lived but couldn't find the house to which it belonged in order to demand that the owner take it down. So instead, they took an AK-47 and fired bullets into the antenna.

During our time in Jalalabad, I witnessed many abuses inflicted on my fellow citizens. For instance, if a person was arrested for nearly any offense, a white van with "The Ministry for Promotion of Virtue and Prevention of Vice" (MPVPV) marked on all four sides would drive around the city informing citizens as to the time, location, and type of punishment to be carried out against the arrestee. The announcements were usually made around noon, and the punishments were carried out in the afternoon as people were about to close their businesses and head for home. The Taliban also brought trucks and buses for people to climb onto and get a good view of the violence. As there were no sports or any kind of arts allowed for people to enjoy, these public humiliations and punishments became the closest thing to entertainment many Afghans had in their lives.

But in Herat, although the Taliban had banned television and music, most people still watched movies and listened to music secretly in their homes. They put very thick blankets on their windows to stop the sound from seeping out of the room and sat close to their TV sets so they could keep the volume low. Usually, one family member stood outside the house to watch for the Taliban. Eventually, we also had a TV and a CD player in our home.

Across the city, there were hundreds of Turkish steam baths (also known as hammams in the majority of Muslim countries) for public bathing. They ran diesel powered generators for several hours in the evening, each providing electricity to around a hundred houses. I remember that *Ek Rishta*, a family movie from India's Bollywood, was the first one we watched during the Taliban regime of pre-2001. When we couldn't find new movies, we would watch the same one repeatedly. I would guess that we watched *Ek Rishta* more than twenty times.

Since it borders Iran in the west and Turkmenistan in the north, Herat had been a business hub for many years. There was a tacit feeling there, or perhaps more of a hope, that the Taliban would not disrupt the business of citizens as long as they abided by the Taliban's rules. However, one morning, the people of Herat awoke to find bodies hanging at seven squares in the city. It was said that the deceased were of Hazara ethnicity, and they were executed for plotting a coup against the Taliban.

In addition to all the stringent rules enforced by the Taliban, two incidents deeply saddened the Afghan people while also gaining international attention: the execution of former President Najibullah in September 1996, and the destruction of the two statues of Buddha in the city of Bamiyan in March 2001. Najibullah, more commonly known as Dr. Najib, served as the President of Afghanistan from 1987 until 1992, when he was forced to resign due to mounting pressure by the UN to hand over power to the mujahideen.

He sought refuge at the UN headquarters in Kabul until the Taliban captured the city and brutally tortured and then hanged him and his brother near the presidential palace. Clearly, one of the reasons that President Ashraf Ghani fled the country on August 15, 2021, just before the Taliban entered Kabul, was that he was terrified of facing the same fate as Dr. Najib.

The two statues of Buddha were constructed circa 600 AD and were considered a UNESCO World Heritage Site. One was fifty-five meters tall and the other one was thirty-eight meters tall. It was said that after the world heard about the Taliban's intention to destroy the statues, UNESCO asked Pakistan's then-President Parvez Musharraf to stop Mullah Omar, the Taliban's Supreme Leader, from doing so. (Pakistan was one of the three countries, including Saudi Arabia and the UAE, that had recognized the Taliban's government in Afghanistan).

"So many great Muslims crossed this land. No one destroyed them. What is your reason for doing so?" Musharraf's representative asked Mullah Omar.

"They might not have had the right tools to destroy them. But I have tanks," Mullah Omar replied.

It was also reported that after a number of scientists approached the Taliban to ask for permission to inspect the statues and repair them if needed, Mullah Omar ordered them to be destroyed because, according to him, the world did not care about millions of living people in need of urgent humanitarian aid, but they cared very much for non-living statues.

CHAPTER THREE
9/11 AND THE OCCUPATION

*At Azada Jirga (Open Discussion), a TV program jointly
run by the BBC and RTA (radio and television of
Afghanistan), Kabul, Afghanistan, 2015.*

At the time of the 9/11 attacks, there was no television broadcasting in Afghanistan. People followed the events of Afghanistan and the world via BBC and VOA (Voice of America) radio broadcasts in Pashto and Dari languages. Because I was a kid and not interested in listening to the news, it was only after I had enrolled at school and learned English that I was aware of the fact that the U.S. had invaded Afghanistan because of the 9/11 attacks.

When the Taliban's regime was toppled in late 2001, I worked at a store in a food market. One day, an old man with a small child brought ten boxes of batteries that were used for hand-held radios over to the store in a pushcart. Although one of the boxes was stolen while he was dropping them off, he told my boss that I had already taken it inside the store. The box was too heavy for me to lift, and my boss told him that if I had taken the box inside the store, there should have been ten boxes, but there were only nine. The man said he would go the Taliban and complain.

I was young and got angry quickly. "I don't care. Go and tell Mullah Omar," I told him, referring to the leader and founder of the Taliban movement.

Around an hour later, a Taliban member came in with a stick in his hand, but when he noticed that I was a teenager, he said to my boss, "Peacefully resolve your problem with this man or I will come tomorrow and detain your boy."

The following day, I was staring at the gate that was right across from the store, worried that a Taliban member might show up at any minute. A guard used to sit at the gate at all times but that day, he wasn't there. At one point, I noticed that the people on the street suddenly began running, and I was afraid that they would rush into the market and loot it. Therefore, I ran over to the gate and closed it. Half an hour later, we were told that the mujahideen had taken control of the city and the Taliban had escaped. My boss and I were so happy.

At the time of the October 7, 2001 invasion of Afghanistan, the Taliban's positions in Herat were also bombed. It seemed that they knew the exact locations of the Taliban's weapons caches and ammunition depots. During the day, B-52 bombers were clearly visible in the sky and at night, air and missile strikes on ammunition depots created scenes similar to fireworks on New Year's Eve. The day after the invasion began, my brothers and I went to Shahr-e-Naw, the most popular section of downtown Herat, and witnessed a long-awaited and emotionally moving scene. People had taken out their old cassette players and photos of Indian movie actors and actresses, and some had even shaved their beards. They were enjoying freedom after many long years of fear and suppression.

Initially, the invasion was not considered an occupation, but more as a unique opportunity for Afghans to prosper and for millions of Afghan refugees in Iran and Pakistan to return to their homeland. At first, everything seemed to be going in the right direction. However, the fighting soon moved from rural areas into the cities where suicide attacks targeting foreign troops resulted in a significant number of civilian casualties.

As the war continued from year to year, more and more civilians perished. When investigations into the 9/11 attacks revealed that none of the perpetrators were Afghan and that most of them had traveled to Pakistan multiple times, Afghans started asking crucial questions and reconsidering their loyalties and options. Years later, the killing of Osama Bin Laden in Pakistan in 2011 by U.S. Navy SEALs supported general suspicions that Pakistan was the main safe haven for the Taliban and other terrorist groups, and that the focus of the war on terror should shift towards that country.

Pakistan, of course, repeatedly denied all allegations. Then, Mullah Akhtar Mansour, the second leader of the Taliban who had replaced Mullah Omar after his death in 2013, was killed by a U.S. drone strike on Pakistani soil. Besides, Pakistani officials themselves confirmed the existence of the Taliban leadership in the city of Quetta, and yet the world still turned a blind eye on Pakistan's involvement in the war in Afghanistan. Even worse, the airstrikes carried out by the U.S. and other foreign forces across the country proved counterproductive; the Taliban sheltered in people's houses and used children as human shields, which resulted in more and more civilian casualties. The survivors of these attacks often then became Taliban sympathizers who later volunteered for suicide bombings, ostensibly to revenge the deaths of their loved ones.

On the other hand, the military invasion in October 2001 was quickly followed by the West's intention to rebuild Afghanistan, and the military campaign to keep the bad guys at bay was simultaneously supported with construction projects across the country. Shuttered schools and universities were reopened, and new ones were built whenever and wherever possible. Millions of students again attended school, and English language and computer skills were heavily promoted, especially in the larger cities. A *Loya Jirga* (Grand Assembly) was convened in 2004 to conceive and construct a new constitution for Afghanistan, which was one of the biggest steps toward democracy in the history of the country.

Soon, thousands of Afghan refugees returned home from Pakistan and Iran, bringing years of higher education and experience with them to a war-torn but hopeful Afghanistan. Most of them felt a sense of ownership after many years of hardship in neighboring countries. Private television channels quickly began broadcasting, bringing news, information, and entertainment to the populace. The Disarmament, Demobilization, and Reintegration (DDR) program helped the new Afghan government and foreign forces gather weapons from people across Afghanistan in exchange for money, education, and jobs.

Once again, Afghanistan established relations with the outside world, and for the first time in its history, Afghanistan held elections so that the people could choose their president and representatives for a parliament and provincial councils. Foreign scholarships were offered to thousands of Afghan students.

In the more urban areas, love marriages began replacing arranged marriages as the norm. Sports became a source of national pride, which resulted in significant achievements for the country. Afghanistan's cricket team, for instance, became a full member of the International Cricket Council (ICC) in less than a decade and played at multiple World Cups, something that had taken around half a century for some other countries to achieve.

Afghan players were soon commanding huge salaries from cricket franchises around the world. Rashid Khan, Afghanistan's famous slow bowler, was paid five hundred thousand dollars in 2017 and over $2 million in 2022 by the Indian Premier League (IPL). Tens of Afghan cricket players are still playing for various franchises around the globe. In addition, Afghanistan's robot-making team, which consisted of five girls from Herat province, made significant achievements at several world events.

Multiple mobile phone companies invested in Afghanistan and soon millions of people were connected with one another across the country. Access to internet made trade and banking easier for Afghan companies to establish business relationships and partnerships, and multiple airlines began operations, flying from Afghanistan to destinations around the globe. More than three hundred thousand ANDSF members, among them thousands of women, were trained and served across Afghanistan.

Industrial ports opened in major cities and employed thousands of people.

Conversely, the support of the international community brought with it a significant amount of intervention in Afghanistan's domestic affairs, from appointing military commanders, governors, and ministers, to the development and endorsement of internal laws, to empowering warlords and to strengthening political opposition groups against the government.

Afghanistan is a diverse country from all aspects and its people belong to numerous ethnic groups. Generally, Pashtons who speak Pashto are located in the eastern and southern parts of the country, while Tajiks who speak Dari are situated in northern and western Afghanistan. Hazaras belong to a few central provinces and the Uzbeks come from a number of provinces in northern Afghanistan. Although over the past twenty years democracy helped Afghans make countless significant achievements, it also took away from them what was probably the most important element of their life—unity.

First, Afghans were divided under the pretext of ethnic balance, dictated by the West, so that an inclusive government could be established. If a minister was Pashton, his deputies were supposed to be Tajik and Hazara. This fraction existed within the ranks of the higher echelons of the ANDSF as well. The 207th Corps of the Afghan National Army (ANA) where I worked as an interpreter/translator for over four years, had a Tajik commander while his deputy was Hazara, and his chief of staff was Pashton. The idea of sharing the power among all ethnic groups of Afghanistan was good, but the way it was practiced created problems. For example, on various occasions, an incompetent officer of the relevant ethnicity was appointed to a very high position. In other instances, such a position remained vacant for years.

The problem got more serious at the time of the 2014 presidential election and beyond. The gap between the different ethnic groups widened because the candidates did more to divide the people than to unite them.

Anytime a political leader nominated himself for the elections, he chose the two vice-presidents from the other ethnic groups (rather than his own) in order to get votes from all the other ethnic groups. Hamid Karzai, who the West installed as the new leader of Afghanistan after the Taliban were ousted in late 2001, ruled for over thirteen years (one year as chairman of the interim administration, two years as the interim president, and two five-year terms as president-elect). He was Pashton by ethnicity, and his vice-presidents were Tajik and Hazara.

The vice-presidents of Ashraf Ghani, also a Pashton, in his first term were Hazara and Uzbek, but he had appointed a Tajik special envoy for himself (in order to win the votes of Tajiks too). In his second term, his vice-presidents were Tajik and Hazara, but he appointed an Uzbek special envoy for himself (in order to win the votes of Uzbeks as well). The main opposition candidate in all four presidential elections, Abdullah Abdullah was Tajik. In the 2019 elections, his vice-presidents were Uzbek and Hazara, and he appointed a Pashton chief executive to his team (to get votes from Pashtons too).

Furthermore, the outcomes of the last two presidential elections were both disputed by Ashraf Ghani and Abdullah Abdullah. The 2014 presidential election did not have a winner in the first round, leading to a second round in which the two front runners, Ashraf Ghani and Abdullah Abdullah, competed against each other. When Ghani was declared the winner, Abdullah challenged the results. Months passed, but the problem remained unresolved until John Kerry, then-U.S. Secretary of State, visited Kabul and asked both leaders to share the power.

Therefore, Afghanistan got a "National Unity Government" (NUG) with *two* presidents that disagreed on nearly every issue—from fighting the Taliban, to the peace process, to attending the UN's annual session, and to participating in any international conference on Afghanistan. Eventually, the two "leaders" agreed to appoint new commissioners to Afghanistan's election commissions—the Independent Election Commission (IEC), and the Independent Electoral Complaints Commission (IECC)—so that any chance of fraud would be prevented at the time of the next elections.

After the 2019 presidential elections, Ashraf Ghani was declared the winner, but Abdullah Abdullah once again disputed the outcome. On the exact same day that Ashraf Ghani was taking the oath of office, his rival, Abdullah Abdullah, held a separate oath ceremony for himself right next to the presidential palace.

Under mounting international pressure, they again agreed to share the power, with Ghani as the president and Abdullah as the chairman of the newly established High Council for National Reconciliation, but the disputes continued unabated. By positioning the two leaders against each other, the international community, and above all the U.S., weakened the government and divided Afghans. It should have been *either* Ghani or Abdullah, with no grey area regarding official status and final say on matters of serious importance.

The two leaders, and by extension their followers, pulled Afghanistan in opposing directions until they eventually tore the fabric of the country apart. Other public figures, among them former warlords and members of the parliament, were no different from Karzai, Ghani or Abdullah. Additionally, for over a decade into the war on terror in Afghanistan, the U.S. military had two missions—to fight the Taliban and Al-Qaeda, and to train and equip the ANDSF. They were accompanied by Afghan interpreters like me who often came from different parts of the country, which meant that sometimes they didn't speak the language of the local population or understand their mores and rituals. For instance, it is considered wrong in the Afghan culture to enter a woman's bedroom or search a woman's closet. In some rural areas, even a woman's husband is not allowed to touch his wife's clothes, much less remove them from a bag.

Sometimes, a small issue such as this could lead to catastrophic incidents. For example, men in southern Afghanistan dress similarly to the Taliban. If an interpreter is not familiar with the area, he can easily mistake local residents for Taliban militants. Additionally, it was common among villagers to gather in the house of the village leader whenever foreign forces were carrying out operations in their village, but often the foreign forces were unaware of this routine. When Coalition Forces used thermal imagery in their surveillance planes to look for the enemy, and they reported to their ground troops that large groups were gathered at a single location, the only person confirming the intelligence was the interpreter. If the interpreter wasn't aware of local rituals and practices, he might confirm the group as the "enemy." Only after an airstrike had killed the group would it become known that it consisted only of innocent women and children.

Even units that partnered with the ANDSF could make fatal mistakes due to a lack of knowledge regarding the local culture and the tribal nuances of a region. One such incident happened on August 21, 2008 in Shindand District of Herat province when I was working as an interpreter/translator for Major General (Two-Star) Jalandar Shah Behnam, the 207th Corps Commander of ANA. The Italian adviser to the Corps Commander and I were in his office when he got a phone call about multiple air airstrikes and a large number of civilian casualties in the village of Azizabad. MG Behnam and Major Abdul Jabbar, the commander of Afghan commando forces in Shindand, were immediately summoned to Kabul for investigations.

I learned about the facts of the incident through official channels and media reports in the following days. One of the tribes (Tribe A) in Azizabad had arranged a large religious ceremony known as Khatam in which people from other parts of Shindand also participated. Food is always served during Khatam, so often children will be rushing to the area for meals. A member of another tribe (Tribe B), which had rivalries with Tribe A, worked as an informant for U.S. Special Forces at Shindand Air Base. He alerted the Special Forces that a large group of Taliban militants, including multiple commanders, had gathered in the village to plan attacks on ANDSF and their coalition counterparts. The Special Forces then dispatched a unit of Afghan commandos to verify the existence of the Taliban in the village. It is common for tribal leaders and influential people in Afghanistan to have at least one, if not multiple, armed escorts. In order to protect themselves from their rival tribesmen, some armed men of Tribe A were providing security on the rooftops of their homes.

As I understood it based on various accounts at the time, when the Afghan commandos reached the village, the armed security guards opened fire on them, fearing that the commandos were there to arrest their leaders. However, official investigations confirmed that the Afghan forces had relayed faulty intelligence to the U.S. Special Forces, who had then requested Close Air Support (CAS). A survivor of the attack later told Radio Free Europe/Radio Liberty that "the district governor has grievances with the residents of Zirkoh [where Azizabad is located]. He gave them [the Americans] wrong information, and they bombed us all and spared nobody." Ninety civilians, including sixty children and fifteen women, were killed in the airstrikes.

It is worth noting that Afghan commandos were not under the command of MG Behnam, and therefore he was soon cleared of all the charges. I consider him to be a great man and believe he was well aware of the long-term implications of the Azizabad incident. He knew that the villagers blamed him for what had happened and that he needed to reach out to them and make sure they understood he had not ordered the airstrikes. But doing so was simply not feasible at the time because his duty was temporarily suspended during the investigations.

Another officer of the ANA, MG Fazl Ahmad Sayar, had been appointed as the 207th Corps commander but when he died in a helicopter crash, MG Behnam was reinstated. On that very same day, he went to Shindand to extend his condolences to the people and let them know that he had been cleared of all the charges because he had not ordered the airstrikes. His Italian adviser, Colonel Ignazio Gamba, and I, also accompanied him on his visit to Shindand.

A summary of the U.S. government's official report regarding the incident reads:

> On the night of August 21-22, 2008, U.S. and Afghan forces entered Azizabad, Shindand District, Herat Province, in order to kill or capture a "High Value Individual" named by the U.S. as Mullah Sadiq. U.S. and Afghan forces approaching the village came under fire. There was a firefight lasting 20 or 30 minutes. The U.S. then called in Close Air Support, which involved an AC-130 gunship and an MQ-9 Reaper UAV (Unmanned Aerial Vehicle/Drone). Airstrikes lasted for two to three hours, and reportedly entailed the dropping of a 500-pound bomb from a drone and shellfire from the gunship's M102 105mm howitzer and 40mm grenades.
>
> For several hours after the airstrikes, the U.S. conducted "site exploitation," during which time evidence was gathered, two wounded civilians were removed for medical assistance, and five men were taken into custody. The detained men included three members of the Afghan National Police and two local residents. They were described as being Taliban members. On August 29 four of the five were released without charge; the fifth spent three months in the U.S. detention facility at Bagram and was then released without charge.
>
> In a press release and media statements during the hours immediately following the operation, the U.S. military denied that there had been any loss of civilian life in Azizabad, but on August 22 a press statement was issued by the U.S. media center at Bagram Air Base admitting that five civilians had been killed and two wounded. Three

separate investigations conducted in the days following by the UN Human Rights Office, the provincial and central government of Afghanistan, and the Afghanistan Independent Human Rights Commission (AIHRC) concluded that from 78 to 92 civilians were killed during the operation, the majority of whom were children.

For several weeks afterwards, U.S. military officials robustly rejected all three alternative accounts. An initial U.S. military inquiry carried out by the Combined Joint Task Force 101 between August 23 and August 29 concluded that no more than five to seven civilians and between 30 to 35 Taliban had been killed. In various media interviews U.S. officials suggested that the villagers were spreading Taliban propaganda. Human Rights Watch interviews with U.S. military personnel, villagers, and nonmilitary investigating officers suggest that this investigation may have been flawed by the lack of U.S. access to the village, as well as a failure to recognize that large numbers of bodies were buried beneath the rubble of the 12 to 14 destroyed and damaged homes.

CHAPTER FOUR
TRANSLATING THE WAR

*Providing simultaneous (real time) interpretation at
Afghanistan's Government Media and Information Center
(GMIC), Kabul, Afghanistan, 2018.*

In 2003, my maternal uncle, who was an engineer, landed a project in Herat where he employed my father. He also implored me and my brothers to enroll in school, which we did. We all studied English as well because everyone stressed its importance for us in the future, particularly if we wanted to pursue higher education. By 2007, I was teaching as an ESL (English as Second Language) teacher and managing an English and computer training center. I loved teaching so much that I was nearly dropped from school in the tenth grade because of extended absences. I was spending all my time with my students!

My oldest brother began working with the U.S. Army combat troops in 2006. Later, he was employed by the U.S. Embassy in Kabul. He served as a Program Specialist with America's Bureau of International Narcotics and Law Enforcement (INL) for over ten years until he relocated to the U.S. in January 2020. In 2009, my older brother started working as an interpreter with the Carabinieri, the national gendarmerie of Italy who trained the Afghan National Police (ANP) in the Adraskan District of Herat province. He then moved to work with U.S. Special Forces as a combat interpreter. In 2015, he was employed as Country Advisor to NATO's Senior Civilian Representative to Afghanistan, and from 2019 to 2020, he served as the Correspondence Director at Afghanistan's State Ministry for Peace. He relocated to the U.S. in October 2020.

In December 2007, my oldest brother returned home on vacation and informed me that the Italian forces at Camp Stone, where hundreds of Coalition Forces advising the ANA were accommodated, were hiring ten interpreters. My parents did not want me to leave home since two of my brothers were already away. The oldest was working for the U.S. Army's 82nd Airborne Division in the southern Kandahar province, and the other was working as a translator and administration officer for a clothes factory in China. But I insisted that I needed to test my English language skills and see whether I could accurately understand a native English speaker. Finally, they agreed, and I passed all the tests with high marks.

In January 2008, I was assigned as a trilingual (Pashto, Dari and English) interpreter/translator to the Italian advisor of ANA's 207th Corps commander. Initially, my family allowed me to work for only a year because I had just finished the tenth grade and still had two more years of high school to complete. They said that the experience of working in an office with high-ranking officials would help me a lot in the future, and they were right.

In terms of the hiring process, in addition to passing a medical exam and a security background check, I needed to pass two language knowledge tests. I still remember that the top of the test paper read, "University of Michigan, English Literature Written Test." This showed that even after seven years of doing business and working in Afghanistan, neither the foreign military nor the corporate leaders had learned how to properly prepare tests for Afghans.

The problem in this regard was that Michigan University's written test for English literature was too difficult to pass for most Afghans (certainly in 2008). Therefore, they ended up hiring as many interpreters as needed even if they failed the written test. Worse than that, they often hired individuals who lacked an insightful cultural awareness of Afghanistan, so they were not able to be effective communicators for such an important job. Besides, often interpreters who spoke Pashto were dispatched to a Dari-speaking region and vice versa. Moreover, I was surprised at the lack of training they provided to new interpreters; most weren't even taught the necessary terms of a basic military vocabulary.

For instance, I had heard that an American officer at Kabul Military Training Centre (KMTC), the main facility for training the ANA, had asked his interpreter to tell the Afghan commander to give extra "magazines" (the part of a gun that holds bullets) to his soldiers so they could defend themselves if ambushed by the Taliban. The interpreter had translated it as "brochures" so the soldiers could "read them and not get bored." I know that seems humorous, but in an atmosphere as politically and culturally charged as Afghanistan, misinterpretation could easily result in the loss of life and/or property.

As years passed, counter-intelligence departments of foreign forces in Afghanistan grew increasingly distrustful of their Afghan interpreters, suspecting that they were leaking classified information to the enemy. I can attest that I personally never saw or heard about any interpreter/translator to have been involved in giving confidential information to the enemy. Still, more and more restrictions were levied on local interpreters such as biannual security interviews for background check, until eventually the DOD issued a directive that required all U.S. Army colonels and above to have Afghan American interpreters (U.S. citizens and permanent residents) who had the necessary security clearances.

More importantly, I once translated at a high-profile meeting in which Afghan authorities and their foreign counterparts were deciding on how to get rid of Hafiz-e-Buland Aab, a notorious Taliban commander who had been threatening a strategic area near Herat international airport for years. It was decided that agents from Afghanistan's National Directorate of Security (NDS), the intelligence services branch of the ANDSF, would disguise themselves as street vendors selling vegetables so they could clandestinely eliminate him when he left his home. The operation was successful—they got the "big fish."

Meanwhile, my older brother had returned from China and was teaching English in downtown Herat. The two of us look very much alike and somehow, someone mistakenly informed Hafiz's militants that the person teaching English was me. Given that they planned to murder my brother, this mistake truly could have had very dire consequences for us. By coincidence, one of my brother's students heard about the plan and immediately informed him.

"That is not me," my brother told his student. "You see me teaching here all day. How is it possible that I work at two different places at one time? Please, tell them that I will meet with them myself so they know that they are following the wrong person." The idea worked and they quit following us both. Before that incident, I went home once a week, but after I heard about the threat, I visited my family far less frequently.

In 2010, as I was about to resign my position and return to school, I had the opportunity to transfer from the Italian forces to the U.S. Army which gave me the opportunity to work at night and attend school during the day. I worked with American forces for more than two years. After graduation from high school, I was accepted into Kabul University's Law and Political Science Faculty. For the next four years, I left the professional world behind and embarked on concentrated academic studies.

Upon my university graduation in 2017, I tried to find a job in the field of law but failed to get anything. Basically, to acquire a job in the government, one had to grease the machine with large sums of money or have connections with officials at the highest levels of authority. The reality of bribes being offered in exchange for legal government work was an open secret. Job security was another challenge because whenever a new president was elected, most government officials and employees were fired by the new administration. And since most high-ranking positions were traded for money, they were soon replaced by anyone who could offer the most substantial bribe. Also, when the government would announce the availability of jobs, nearly all of them would be in Taliban-controlled areas.

Given this reality, and with over four years of previous experience, my only option was to continue in the field of interpretation/translation, and I secured a position as Senior Interpreter/Reviser at the headquarters of the RSM in Afghanistan. The degree undoubtedly helped me secure a much better job, and with significantly higher pay this time around.

With respect to my personal life, my wife, Shazia, and I were married in October 2018. Shazia is a tough woman, a great mother, and a caring partner. She also hails from Paktia, the province where I was born. She has two brothers and three sisters and is the fourth child of her parents. I first saw her on our engagement day. Our daughter, Lima, was born in August 2019.

Although we had an arranged marriage, my family and that of my wife had known each other for over half a century. Her two aunts were married to two friends of my father. My grandparents, and those of my wife, lived next door in Kabul before the civil war, and when most people from Kabul were internally displaced during the civil war, my family and that of my wife lived as neighbors in Jalalabad. In 2010, her cousin studied engineering in Herat, and we became friends. When my family moved to Kabul in 2013, her cousin took me and my older brother to multiple wedding parties which my wife's family also attended. Last year, when she was watching the movie of her older sister's wedding, she discovered that my brother and I were also in attendance!

During my second employment as an linguist with foreign forces from 2017 to 2021, my main responsibility was to verify the work of other junior colleagues to make sure there were no mistakes in the documents they translated from English to Dari or Pashto and vice versa. Also, I provided simultaneous (real time) and consecutive interpretation at high level meetings attended by Afghan officials and their U.S./NATO counterparts.

My native language is Pashto, but I grew up and studied in areas where most people spoke Dari. Therefore, I am fluent in both, which helped me get hired nearly every time I applied for a job as a linguist. It was usually with a private contracting company such as Aegis, Titan, DynCorp, and MEP who hired interpreters for foreign forces in Afghanistan. In 2008, I began with Aegis, but later shifted to MEP because the former lost the contract with the DOD, and from 2017 to 2021, I was directly hired by the RSM in Afghanistan.

The office where I worked till July 2021 provided three distinct types of interpretation: consecutive, liaison, and simultaneous. Consecutive interpretation was the most common form. One party spoke for a minute or so, the interpreter translated it, and the party continued speaking for another minute or so followed by the interpreter's translation. Liaison interpretation was required when an issue was discussed with the interpreter on the phone, and then the message would be translated in the target language to the opposite party. Simultaneous interpretation, also known as real-time interpretation, was the most challenging, and was only used at high level meetings in order to safe time. I learned the skill during my first employment with foreign forces (2008-2012) and improved it during my second employment (2017-2021), and then helped many colleagues acquire that capability as well.

Later, I was given supervisory responsibilities as per my job description. I checked the exam papers of new hires, briefed them on the work environment, introduced them to other colleagues, and managed their timesheets and leave days. However, as more and more U.S. and other foreign troops began leaving Afghanistan, the Linguistic Services Branch (LSB) at the RSM where I worked had to release some of its staff too, and my Afghan American boss asked me to help him identify those whose services were no longer needed. My boss and I considered all criteria in this regard. We agreed to first release those whose SIVs had been approved. Other matters included, but were not limited to, quality and quantity of work, attendance, previous warnings, etc. Though some of my colleagues provided high quality work and were among the most experienced, our hands were often tied; we needed to make the requisite cuts to staff.

Had we released someone whose SIV case wasn't approved, they would have often found themselves unemployed for long periods, and even worse, lost any guarantee that their SIV application would be approved. Yet, many of those released were upset with our decisions and blamed me for being biased. A few of them even complained to the Counterintelligence (CI) at their security interviews about my behavior, and I was pressed repeatedly on these issues when I had my own security interviews with the CI.

Surprisingly, nearly all who were released as part of the drawdown of foreign forces were Pashton, the same ethnic group as mine and that of my Afghan American boss. Had I been biased, no Pashton colleague of mine would have been released from duty. In each and every case, my boss and I considered the greater good for the LSB staff, and the opportunity for them to eventually emigrate to the U.S. In retrospect, I am quite proud of the fact that most of the people who worked at the LSB during my years there, and who I may have been forced to let go, eventually found their way out of Afghanistan.

In the first few years after the U.S. invasion of Afghanistan, being an interpreter was a good paying job. A small number of Afghans who began working as interpreters right after foreign forces entered the country at the end of 2001 later became millionaires (in dollars) and recently served at the highest level of the Afghan government. In addition to bridging the linguistic gap between foreign troops and locals, interpreters were sometimes given large amounts of dollars (by foreign forces) to purchase things that were urgently needed, or items required for the establishment of ANDSF units, such as furniture and computers.

Some of them priced items at two or even ten times the original cost. As years passed and more foreign forces arrived, the establishment of ANDSF units extended across the country, and most of the supplies needed by foreign forces and the ANDSF were imported from businesses around the world. By that point, many interpreters had become major contractors. They opened logistics companies supplying everything from furniture to computers, gravel to wood, gas to power generators, uniforms to boots, and cars to construction vehicles. A few of them even established private security companies.

One of the issues that really bothered me (and likely irritated every Afghan interpreter/translator who worked with foreigners) was that the public did not like *Tarjuman*, the Dari word for the position we held. They thought that since we worked with the "infidels," we were no different from them because, allegedly, we drank alcohol and never offered prayers. Interpreters were often compared to informants or foreign agents, particularly when they worked with Special Forces. Once, a classmate of mine at Kabul University saw a picture of me in uniform and asked about it. I told him that it was from the time when I was an interpreter with foreign forces.

"You must regret what you have done!" he scolded, but I told him that I was proud of every bit of it.

When the Covid-19 restrictions were enforced, the RSM headquarters in Kabul where I worked went into lockdown, and all local employees (Afghan nationals) were required to remain on the base for months. I was in lockdown twice; the first time for four months and the second time for nearly three months. It was a hard time for my wife Shazia, but she stayed strong. When the execution of journalists, civil society activists, and government officials by the Taliban began in November 2020, she was afraid that I might be targeted for working with foreign forces or by robbers wanting to steal my car. In fact, her concern was quite justified. I was working at the highest level of the U.S. military and NATO forces in Afghanistan, which made me a good target for the insurgents. Also, those working with foreigners, like myself, were known to be paid in dollars, which really incentivized kidnappers.

Though I was never robbed or kidnapped, mainly because of the defensive tactics I had learned at work, the threat of remote-controlled Improvised Explosive Devices (IEDs) was so high in late 2020 and early 2021, that no one felt safe anywhere, at any time. The Taliban began killing journalists and civil society activists and then, after a month or so, started assassinating members of the ANDSF. Then, they shifted to planting bombs in civilian passenger buses and vans.

In early 2021, I missed being hit by an IED by just five minutes. It was planted near the building where I lived and the target was a deputy minister of Afghanistan's Ministry of Telecommunication and Information Technology. I saw a black armored Land Cruiser that arrived to pick him up as I was leaving the area. Five minutes later, my father called to see if I was okay. The deputy minister had to attend a funeral, and he had told his driver to return to the Ministry. Only the driver was killed in the explosion.

The most dramatic and horrifying incident of my career as an interpreter happened in January 2009. An Afghan army battalion had done a great job of providing security for voter registration for the impending presidential election. Major General Fazl Ahmad Sayar, ANA's 207th Corps commander, wanted to visit the battalion in the southwestern Farah province, two hundred miles away, and personally congratulate them on their achievement. He discussed the planning with his Italian advisor, Colonel Ignazio Gamba. Per the Standard Operating Procedure (SOP), foreign military officers and their interpreters were not authorized to fly with Afghan helicopters and/or ride in Afghan vehicles. MG Sayar was supposed to fly with two Russian Mi-17 helicopters of the Afghan Air Force (AAF). Col. Gamba said that he would see if he could get any NATO helicopters to fly with the commander.

As we left Sayar's office, Gamba said, "I have no problem flying with the commander in the Mi-17, but I won't force you to do so."

I replied, "He is a major general of the Afghan Army, and you are a NATO colonel. If you don't have a problem with it, I don't mind either." We then told the commander that we would fly with him in the Mi-17 if NATO did not provide us with our own helicopters.

Now, keep in mind that interpreters were only allowed to let their parents know the barest details regarding where they would be travelling on a mission, with no further details authorized to be shared with anyone. Accordingly, I only told my father that we were going to Farah the following day.

The next morning, the weather was cold and the skies were cloudy. Gamba called and instructed me to call MG Sayar and see if he still wanted to go to Farah. Though I had two mobile phone numbers for the Corps commander, I always preferred to get in touch with his office secretary first, out of respect. I got him on the line, and he said the commander was busy and did not plan on going anywhere. When I informed Gamba of this, he told me to ask if he planned on going there by road. The secretary's response was "negative."

Gamba then called me for the third time, saying, "I know you don't like calling the commander directly, but please call him on his own number and ask him directly if he is going anywhere today."

I again called the secretary and said, "Gamba wants to hear from the commander himself." I heard MG Sayar reply "no" through the secretary's phone so I called Gamba and relayed the information. A few minutes later, Gamba called me and said, "Get ready, you and I are flying out in fifteen minutes."

Gamba's request had been approved and two Spanish Air Force Cougar helicopters flew in from Herat International Airport, twenty miles north of the Corps, and landed at the Corps Helicopter Landing Zone (HLZ) to take us to Farah.

While we were waiting, a single AAF Mi-17 helicopter flew overhead. Gamba remarked, "They said that they could not fly in this weather, so what is this?" As per the SOP, both NATO and Afghan helicopters flew in pairs so that they could support each other in case of any emergency or enemy attack. Moreover, it was Thursday, the first day of the weekend in Afghanistan, and the ANDSF usually practiced training and held mass cleaning sessions on Thursdays.

Accordingly, I said to Gamba, "It could be an exercise. It's Thursday."

In addition to the military assistance, NATO member countries had established a Provincial Reconstruction Team (PRT) in each province in order to expedite the implementation of welfare projects across the country. The PRT in Farah belonged to the U.S. Army. Back then, Farah did not have a standard airport, but the American PRT had multiple HLZs. Also, my oldest brother had recently been transferred from the combat zone in southern Afghanistan to the PRT in Farah. I was happy that I would be able to meet up with him on the trip.

The helicopters flew over Zirkoh, a mountainous area in the Shindand District of Herat province. At one point, the pilots thought it would be easier for them to fly *through* the mountains rather than fly higher and cross over them. But they miscalculated the steepness of the mountains and soon found nearly insurmountable peaks looming before them, one after the next. They tried to pull the nose of the helicopter up, but it was nearly impossible. We had so many close calls that I closed my eyes and prayed to Almighty Allah for forgiveness. But the pilots, somehow, got us through.

When we landed at Farah PRT, I first went to see my brother, but he wasn't there. One of his colleagues said that he had gone on a mission to Gulistan, one of Farah's districts. Then, I went to the dining facility where Gamba awaited. While preparing to eat, I got a call from a colleague who worked with the point of contact of the Italian forces for Afghan interpreters. He asked me if I was alright. A minute later, another colleague called and asked the same question. It wasn't common to call a colleague who was on a mission. Then, Gamba's phone rang. When he hung up, he said in a serious tone, "The Corps commander is missing!"

"No way!" I blurted out. "Three times, he said he wasn't going anywhere!"

After finishing lunch, we both went to see the ANA battalion which consisted of around four hundred officers, noncommissioned officers (NCOs), and soldiers, but there were just two soldiers there. When I asked them where the other personnel were, one of them said, "The Corps commander has gone missing. He was on his way to attend an ANP graduation ceremony in Adraskan and then was coming to visit us. We were told that his helicopter made an emergency landing somewhere near Adraskan. Everyone is out there looking for him."

It turned out there was another event taking place that day that I had no knowledge of. A unit of the ANP was graduating from a training center in the Adraskan District of Herat province, around fifty miles away. A delegation of dignitaries from Kabul was scheduled to attend the ceremony, and Gamba assumed the commander would need to take part in the event. This was why he kept imploring me to determine the commander's travel plans.

Lieutenant Colonel Najibullah of the ANA was the Corps commander's secretary, and he accompanied the commander nearly everywhere he went. I immediately called him to see what had happened, and he confirmed what the soldier in Farah had said. When I asked him why the commander had chosen to fly after he had rejected flying three times earlier in the day, Najibullah said, "He changed his mind at the very last minute."

Then, as we were about to get on board the helicopters to return to Herat, Gamba's deputy called him and said that they had found the Corps commander. I felt so relieved.

On our way back from Farah, around twenty Italian troops joined us. The crew asked me to sit next to the door, which remained open at all times, in order for the helicopter gunner to be watchful of a potential enemy attack. The helicopters flew at a very high altitude and the higher they flew, the colder the weather got. Though I had my body armor, helmet, and gloves on, it was extremely cold because the wind was blowing directly on me.

When we arrived over the 207th Corps area, I saw hundreds of ANA vehicles, including ambulances, entering the compound while the entire personnel of the Corps, over ten thousand people, were standing outside their barracks. Gamba's deputy was waiting for us at the HLZ. As we got off the helicopter, he said, "The Corps commander has been killed." I was shocked. We immediately went to the Corps' Tactical Operation Center (TOC) where the chief of staff of the Corps was grappling with the situation. I saw tears in his eyes. Other officers were also crying. At that moment, my phone rang.

I stepped outside, and when I looked at my phone, there were 131 missed calls and 87 text messages, and the battery was about to die. I later realized that after our helicopters had lifted off from Farah PRT, the news of the death of the commander had spread around the country, and my family was in shock because I had told my father the day before that I would be traveling with him. Though my colleagues and my brother's colleague whom I had met at the PRT had assured my family that I was okay, my father wanted to hear it from me directly. My phone had been ringing all the way from Farah to Herat, but because of the loud noise of the helicopter, I hadn't heard it. I finally talked to my father and reassured him I was safe, and then went back to the TOC.

I said to Gamba, "I am so cold and in deep shock. I need to take a break. I will return as soon as I get a hot shower and calm down a little bit." I asked for his permission to go to my room, and he granted my wish.

MG Fazl Ahmad Sayar, the Corps commander, three of his escorts, his operations and communications officers, and the entire crew of the helicopter had died in the crash. The crew of the second helicopter that was following the commander's helicopter later said that it was suddenly enveloped by thick clouds and as soon as it cleared them, a mountain stood waiting, too large to evade.

Dealing with the aftermath of the incident was challenging. Neither AAF planes nor those from NATO and the U.S. were able to fly from Kabul to Herat for the casualty evacuation (CASEVAC) due to bad weather that night. Therefore, all relevant ceremonies were left for the following morning. There, Major Khan, the commander of a U.S. Marine Forces Special Operations Command (MARSOC) unit was surprised to see me alive. He said, "The first one that crossed my mind was you. You were with the Corps commander at every event. I am happy to see you alive, my friend."

For a few days, I did not sleep well. I had worked closely with all those who had died in the crash. The commander had very friendly escorts. We made jokes and laughed every day when we waited outside the commander's office. The commander himself was very kind. Though he did not smile a lot, he often expressed his kindness. I still remember how he once said to Gamba, "When it comes to an interpreter, I am always lucky. Wherever I am assigned, I find a very good interpreter, and Jamil is one of them."

With regard to the partnership between Coalition Forces and the ANDSF, there were certain issues, but one of them was critical. Though working *shana-ba-shana*, or shoulder to shoulder was a very common motto, often very small issues made Afghan officers question their partnership with the Western allies.

Generally, whenever Coalition Forces visited ANDSF compounds, they only showed their IDs (from inside their vehicles/without getting off) to the guards and went through all the gates without being stopped or searched. However, when ANDSF or other officials of the Afghan government visited Coalition Forces camps for meetings, change of command ceremonies, or other occasions, very strict security procedures were applied. They had to submit a full list of all the vehicles, personnel, and weapons in advance. When they arrived, they were asked to unload their weapons, remove the magazines, and park their vehicles to be searched by K9s.

In April 2008, I accompanied Major General Jalandar Shah Behnam, ANA's 207th Corps commander, to a very important conference in Kabul. On our way back to Herat, the security guards at Kabul Airport, who I believe were from New Zealand, asked MG Behnam to pass through a full body scanner. He was infuriated. He did not want to go through the scanner. It was a matter of honor and dignity for him. Finally, his American advisor, a U.S. Army colonel, solved the problem, and the commander entered the airport without being scanned.

"What do these people think of themselves? It is our country, and I am a major general of this country. Do they think I am carrying explosives? That is ridiculous," MG Behnam later told me when we got on the plane.

The problem was not resolved till the end. When I worked at the RSM headquarters in Kabul (till July 2021), they often invited Afghan authorities to official meetings and other events. One of the requirements was that they had to have their A4-size paper IDs, known as *tazkeras*, on them. However, when more and more people obtained electronic ID cards, the rule changed and paper *tazkeras* were not valid any longer for entering the HQ, but Coalition Forces hadn't informed their Afghan counterparts of the change in the regulations. Though most of those who visited the HQ were biometrically enrolled on the security systems, they were not allowed to go in, and all the efforts put into the arrangements went in vain. Such incidents sometimes made Afghan officials believe that the Coalition Forces did not consider them to be reliable partners.

Another issue was that American troops rotated annually and the rotation cycle for other NATO forces was six months. In a country like Afghanistan, it is nearly impossible for any foreign troops to get to know the terrain, the people and their culture, much less how to properly train their local allies in such a short period of time. From my own experience of working with Italian and American troops, I can say that as soon as they got to know the way of life of the Afghan people and befriended with them, they were replaced by new units. As a result, the training of ANDSF that should have completed in a few years took nearly two decades. Worse than that, often newly deployed units could not differentiate between the local allies and the enemies, and would not listen to their Afghan interpreters either. This sometimes led to terrible incidents resulting in casualties for the civilians and the Coalition Forces.

Worst of all, sometimes, lack of cultural awareness led to tragic incidents involving the death of senior officers of the Coalition Forces as well as ANDSF. One such incident happened in April 2011 when an Afghan pilot of the AAF killed nine Americans (eight officers and a contractor). It was said that the pilot was infuriated when the American trainers repeatedly used the word "F**K" in their conversations though it wasn't clear whether they were talking about their Afghan students or the Taliban.

On the other hand, there were often officers on both sides who were really impressive, but faced unpleasant ends to their missions. One of them was Italian Army Colonel Ignazio Gamba who advised ANA's 207th Corps commander. In many ways, he was different from other foreign officers. Every day, before going to the Corps commander's office, he would explain to me all the issues he wanted to discuss with the commander. He wanted me to fully understand all relevant matters so I could best relay them to the commander. Therefore, he always kept me fully informed.

Gamba was always friendly to everyone, and even joked with Afghan soldiers. Almost everyone in the ANA knew him well, and he took good care of the Afghan linguists assigned to the Italian forces. Before his tour ended, he asked me if there was anything he could do for us (the interpreters).

All Afghan interpreters stayed at *Terp Village*, a small compound of around thirty barracks in an area between the Afghan and Coalition Forces compounds. The linguists working for the American forces had their own barracks, but those working for the Italians resided in barracks that also belonged to the U.S. Army, meaning we could be kicked out at any time. Therefore, I asked Gamba to build separate barracks for the interpreters working for the Italian forces, and in less than a month, the barracks were ready.

Unfortunately, toward the end of Gamba's mission, a terrible incident nearly undermined all his good work. In mid-2009, a convoy of Italian forces opened fire on a civilian Afghan vehicle, killing four people. There were three Italian units in Herat at the time and they all operated in similar armored military vehicles called *Lince* (pronounced *Leenche)*.

In order to protect themselves against possible Vehicle Borne Improvised Explosive Devices (VBIEDs), or simply put, car bombs, all foreign troops were advised that the easiest way to avoid civilian casualties, especially in the case of any suspicious vehicle approaching any foreign forces convoy or military base, was that they were to first fire a few warning shots into the air. Then, they would fire more warning shots on both sides of the approaching vehicle, and lastly, they would aim at the tires to eliminate the threat.

A civilian vehicle was traveling from Herat to Farah after a shopping trip for an upcoming wedding. It seemed that the driver had ignored or probably hadn't heard the warning shots. Meanwhile, two different convoys of Italian forces were out on the road at that exact time and one of them was Gamba's. Though his team denied any involvement in the incident, they were blamed for the tragic loss of lives because it had happened in an area where the other unit did not usually have any business. Gamba was very upset because even his wife back in Italy thought that his men had committed the crime. Later, after becoming a Brigadier General (One-Star), Gamba was assigned as the commander of all Coalition Forces in Western Afghanistan. He is now a Lieutenant General (Three-Star) in the Italian Army and serves as the commander of Alpini troops, and I am still in touch with him.

The other officer was Jalandar Shah Behnam, then a Major General of the ANA and commander of the 207th Corps. He was from Panjshir, the stronghold of former mujahideen commander Ahmad Shah Massoud. Before joining the mujahideen ranks, Behnam was a decorated officer in Afghanistan's Soviet-backed armed forces. Besides being a very intelligent commander, he was a good leader too. He was very tough on his subordinates because he believed that was how things should be run in the military, particularly at a time of war. He also kept in contact with other branches of the government and knew very well how to engage with civilians.

In August 2008, he was removed from the 207th Corps for a short period of time because of an air bombardment by the U.S. Air Force in the Shindand District, Herat province. During that time, Fazl Ahmad Sayar, another Major General of the ANA, was serving as the Corps commander. Like Behnam, MG Sayar also had served in the Soviet-backed armed forces of Afghanistan before joining Ahmad Shah Massoud's mujahideen group, and he also belonged to Panjshir. But Sayar wasn't as intelligent as Behnam.

Back then, one of the tactics that Taliban militants used was attacking a couple of remote bases simultaneously.

When reinforcements were sent, the militants ambushed them on their way. One such incident happened when MG Sayar was in charge. An ANA outpost was attacked, and he ordered another unit to go and push back the Taliban attack, but they were ambushed. A dozen Afghan soldiers were killed and around ten others were captured alive. MG Sayar hadn't spent much time in western Afghanistan and therefore did not have good connections with people in the area. He later died in a helicopter crash, and Behnam was brought back in. He soon got in touch with tribal elders in the area and facilitated the release of the Afghan soldiers.

On August 5, 2014, when MG Behnam commanded Marshal Fahim National Defense Academy (MFNDU), an Afghan soldier opened fire on a delegation of U.S. and NATO officers who were visiting the training center, also known as Camp Qargha. As a result, U.S. Army Major General (Two-Star) Harold Greene, the deputy commander of the Combined Security Transition Command–Afghanistan (CSTC-A), was killed and a dozen other U.S. and NATO officers were wounded. Greene was the highest-ranking officer in the American military killed in Afghanistan during the twenty years of the Global War on Terror (GWOT). It was reported then that Behnam was also wounded in the attack. Worse than that, in 2017, his son, an ANA physician, was killed when Taliban militants stormed the ANA hospital. After the Taliban took control of Kabul in August 2021, Behnam and his family were evacuated to Italy.

CHAPTER FIVE
CHAOS AT KABUL AIRPORT

*August 19, 2021: With my family, inside Kabul airport,
after crossing the airport gate, Kabul, Afghanistan.*

t 2:00 p.m. the day after the Taliban assumed power, local Afghan TV stations broadcast footage of thousands of people storming Kabul Airport trying to get on the U.S. military planes that had brought in U.S. Marines for extra security. No one was in control; the Afghan staff had left their jobs the day before. By 3:00 p.m., multiple videos of a C-17—a huge U.S. military plane designed for cargo transportation—went viral. They were filmed from different angles and some of the videos showed up to twenty people clinging to the sides of the plane as it was about to take off. Others showed three people falling to the ground after the plane had lifted off. It was later reported that they had died, and also that some human remains were found in the landing gear compartment of the plane after it had landed in Qatar. Meanwhile, the AWA Advocacy Group started warning SIV applicants not to go to the airport. They said that we should wait until more U.S. Marines were deployed to provide security in and around the airport.

The evacuation, which was initially called the relocation of those who had worked for the U.S. over the previous twenty years, had actually begun several months earlier in the beginning of 2021, but the process was very slow and fraught with problems and red tape. Normal SIV process stages included applying for the SIV, receiving Chief of Mission (COM) approval, an interview at the U.S. Embassy, taking a medical exam, receiving a visa, and booking the tickets. However, by the time of Kabul's fall into the clutches of the Taliban, the U.S. had only relocated a few hundred SIV applicants who had qualified earlier.

A major problem was that many SIV applicants lacked the money needed to complete the process. The medical exam cost $450 and the plane ticket could run up to $1,200 per person. Most of the applicants had lost their jobs after former U.S. President Donald Trump ordered a significant reduction of American troops in Afghanistan. Many people desperate to leave as soon as possible because of threats to their lives would sell all of their belongings to raise the necessary funds, while others would borrow from relatives and friends. Everyone in Afghanistan who had worked for foreign troops was frantic after Kabul fell once again to the Taliban.

That evening, U.S. Marines and Zero units (which consisted of hundreds of local Afghans trained and paid by the

CIA for night raids and clandestine missions) began moving people out of Kabul Airport. The Taliban were asked by the Marines to stop people from approaching the airport gates while the Marines and the Zero teams cleared necessary areas inside. Though they tenuously succeeded in quelling the chaos inside the buildings, people did not leave the streets around the airport.

Meanwhile, videos of Taliban members roaming the streets of Kabul, firing in the air to disperse crowds and beating people indiscriminately, raised the specter of the Taliban era before 9/11. I knew that even if I were to escape execution for working with foreign forces, my little daughter would not be able to attend school or work when she grew up, my wife would lose many freedoms, and I would need to find employment in a completely new field. The problem was that with the U.S. Embassy closed and all the chaos around the airport, I had no idea how to get my family out of the country. And the clock was ticking.

On the third day of the fall of Afghanistan, Firooz Farjam, a friend of mine in Italy, texted me on WhatsApp. "Get in touch with Fraidoon," he said. "He and others are coordinating with the Italians to get out. Try to join them."

He was referring to another friend whom I had worked with during my employment with the Italian forces from January 2008 to July 2009 at Camp Stone, a Coalition Forces base in Afghanistan's western Herat province. I realized that it would be extremely difficult, if not impossible, for the U.S. Embassy personnel now operating from within the airport to arrange for the safe and orderly evacuation of hundreds of U.S. citizens and Green Card holders (permanent residents), much less thousands of SIV applicants and their families. Therefore, I saw the Italian evacuation as perhaps our only escape route. I thought that I would process my SIV case in Italy later, and then hopefully we could move to the U.S.

I called Fraidoon, who was still in Kabul, and asked him about the process, and to include my name if possible. His response wasn't encouraging. He said, "I will give your name to our representative, but it may be too late for you now." The representative of the Italian interpreters did not remember my name because it had been more than a decade since I had left working with the Italian forces. He would need to meet me in person before any assistance would be offered.

The following morning, on August 18, 2021, the fourth day of the Taliban in Kabul, I called my father-in-law to make sure they were okay. I told him that my wife and I would visit them in an hour to say our goodbyes in case any of us had to leave suddenly and there wasn't enough time to see each other. The Taliban announced that their leadership had forgiven those who had worked in the Afghan government and/or for the "invaders," their preferred term for all foreign forces in Afghanistan. There seemed to be a lull in Taliban retribution or retaliation, so I felt a little safer leaving the house.

I was also hungry for any news about the Italian evacuation that morning. Firooz, who had moved to Italy with his family in early 2021, had spent more than a month in quarantine before they were resettled in a government-sponsored house of their own. With him in mind, I left to run some errands. When I returned home and checked my phone, there was an evacuation notice from the Italians.

"Get to the eastern gate of the airport quickly!" the message read in Dari. I excitedly shared the news with my family.

My father and two siblings were astonished, happy, and at the same time, sad. They couldn't believe that more than a decade after leaving my job with the Italian forces, they would still evacuate me and my family. Mostly, they were relieved about the fact that we would be out of harm's way. But they were also worried that something bad could happen to us at the airport, and disappointed that our family wouldn't be around for my younger brother's wedding. He was engaged to my wife's younger sister and their wedding was scheduled to take place in two weeks. I had personally booked a hall for them and had also printed the invitation cards.

We started packing, keeping it to only what we really needed. We prepared one fairly large rolling bag and two backpacks. Mobile phones and chargers, medicine, snacks, a few bottles of water, and money (U.S. dollars) were on the top of the list. Following that, I called my father-in-law and asked him to bring his family to a spot along the road to the airport so that we could meet for a quick farewell. I also called a friend who had a taxi and asked him to come and take us to the airport. We left the house at 8:45 a.m. and met my in-laws a few minutes later. We didn't have much time—just a few minutes to say our goodbyes by the side of the road. My friend Fraidoon and his family linked up with us too.

After crossing multiple Taliban checkpoints, we got to the airport's eastern gate at around 9:30 a.m. As thousands of people surged, U.S. Marines and forces from multiple other countries, including Italians soldiers, were holding the line at the airport entrance. Interpreters who had worked for the Italian military were arriving one after the next with their families. However, our representative wasn't there.

After making some calls, I learned that he and some others were lost, though I had given them clear instructions on how to get to the airport. My wife and daughter were in the taxi in tears. I asked the driver to move to the shade as we might have to wait for hours. People kept pouring into the area in front of the gate, desperate to get in.

Then, five Taliban militants riding on a military Ford Ranger Light Tactical Vehicle (LTV) arrived. The vehicle still carried ANP marks. One of them, a teenager carrying an AK-47, stayed in the back of the LTV. The other four started pushing people back from the gate, ostensibly to help the U.S. Marines and other foreign forces restore order. They shouted at people and threatened them with their rifles.

The uneasy truce among the Taliban and the U.S. Marines grew as hours passed. At one point, I noticed that a U.S. Marine and a Taliban militant were standing no more than three feet away from each other on a concrete barricade near the airport entrance. I still remember that the Marine offered the Taliban militant an energy drink, but the Taliban militant did not take it, apparently believing that it was *haram*, meaning Islam prohibited it. I really wanted to take a picture of that scene, but out of fear that the Taliban militant would likely break my mobile phone if not shoot me for doing so, I decided against it.

After a two-hour search, Fraidoon and I finally found our representative at another gate. He was with ten more interpreters and their families. The Taliban militants at this gate were much harsher than those at the eastern gate, firing sprays of AK-47 bullets into the air every five minutes to disperse the crowd. The shots were very frightening, especially for the women and children. It was around 12:15 p.m. when we returned to the eastern gate, but when our representative called the Italian Point of Contact (POC), he was told that the Italians were done for the day and that the U.S. Marines wouldn't move any more people inside as there wasn't enough space.

This wasn't what we were expecting. Our group of interpreters and their families numbered over three hundred people. Many were from Herat province and had no relatives in Kabul. They had been sleeping in hotels. They could not go back because there were Taliban militants everywhere now. Therefore, we tried to persuade the Italians to at least get us inside the airport, saying we would wait inside the airport for days if we had to. The Italian POC finally agreed to get our representative and his family in so they could finalize the manifest. I personally advised others to let only the representative go but not his family, because if he had the choice to leave without us, he wouldn't do so without them. The Italian POC didn't agree. He wanted both the representative and his family inside the airport ASAP.

The initial plan was that we all would be evacuated the following morning in three flights, but at 6:00 p.m., our representative called to inform us that the flights might be cancelled, the hangar was full, and there was no space for any more people inside. He said we could either go home or spend the night outside the gate. Then he said, "The Italians want me and my family to leave tonight. Unfortunately, I won't be able to help you beyond this point. The second person listed at the top of the manifest is now your representative. He knows what to do." This was what I had feared might happen.

Some folks from Kabul left and went back to their homes while those from Herat chose to stay. I talked with my wife about our options and we agreed we should stay because it was highly likely that the Taliban would establish more checkpoints in the city, so we might not be able to get back to the airport the following day if we left. I asked the taxi driver to call his wife and tell her that he would have to stay with us until morning. Fraidoon and his family also decided to stay.

Meanwhile, I got a message on WhatsApp from Ignazio Gamba, my old friend of the Italian army whom I worked with in 2009. He wanted to see if I was okay and whether I had made it out of Afghanistan safely. I wrote him back and let him know what was going on.

I also got an email from John Schofield, a former U.S. Army captain with whom I had worked in 2010-11. He was worried about me, but I didn't know how he could really help us because there wasn't an organized evacuation system in place. Mirwais Rahin, my boss at RSM, also kept in touch to make sure I was okay, but he had already left in June (two months before the withdrawal) and was now living in Turkey. There wasn't much he could do for us.

I then went to observe the U.S. Marines to better understand how the process was likely to unfold. They instructed SIV applicants to come the following morning. However, I noticed that they also were allowing family members and relatives of U.S. citizens, Green Card holders, and Afghan nationals with U.S. visas to pass through the gate, even if they (the family members) did not have any documents. That gave me the idea of a *Plan B* just in case the Italian evacuation didn't happen the following morning. I called my younger brother back home and asked him to print out my SIV documents and bring them to the airport (and to bring us some food too).

A senior citizen whose house was in the vicinity of the airport gate graciously offered to let our women and children sleep in his house and said that we could also use his washroom.

"It's been like this for the last four days. I open the door of my house to these people because I understand them," he told us.

My father and father-in-law came with my brother to see how we were doing, and my wife had called my sister and asked for another bag of clothes, which my brother brought as well. Before they left, I gave my brother the power bank for my mobile phone to fully charge and bring back to us early the next morning.

It is worth mentioning that during the fourteen hours we spent outside the airport gate, I saw more than a hundred passenger buses carrying people to the gate. Each convoy was escorted by two vehicles of armed Taliban militants, one in the front and the other in the back, and one Taliban militant was guarding the door of each bus. Since they did not have any signs, it wasn't clear to me who the people on the buses were, but their movement was definitely coordinated by the Taliban.

When they arrived, the U.S. Marines formed two lines on both sides of the buses in order to stop other people from cutting into the lines and merging with them.

Just after midnight, we received another phone call from our representative, who said, "The three flights for tomorrow morning have been canceled. The Americans want to evacuate as many of their people as possible. One flight is taking off shortly and there will be two more flights in two days' time." He then left for Italy. I had tried to warn everyone this would happen!

71

Everyone, especially those who had stayed the night behind the airport gate, wanted to be on that first flight. The second person listed on the manifest, who was now responsible for coordinating with the Italian POC, said, "The first hundred people on the manifest should go first. The second and third groups should go in the next two days, in that order."

Not all of us agreed with him. They had generated the manifest in such a way that the first hundred people were from a particular ethnic group. I recommended that there be people from the beginning, middle, and end of the manifest among those getting on the first flight.

"You say so because your name is at the end," said our new organizer while angrily pointing at me. This was true — my family and I *were* among the last people added to the manifest. I told him that I would wait for the last flight, but he was now harboring ill will towards me. We agreed to disagree, and when I left the meeting, I immediately went to see if we might make it through the gate by showing my SIV documents to the U.S. Marines.

Though it was after midnight, people were still coming in droves and pushing towards the gate. I had a small bag in my hand that contained our passports and IDs, my SIV documents, and our money. I could not risk losing it in the crowd, but my wife and daughter were asleep, and I did not want to wake them up before I had a confirmation that we could make it through the gate. Therefore, I left the small bag and my phones with the taxi driver (who was, thankfully, a trusted friend), and left with only my wallet, which contained fifteen hundred Afghanis (then equal to around twenty dollars) and two small passport-size photos of my wife and daughter.

After pushing for ten minutes, I got close enough to the crossing line to observe how things worked. The Marines were shouting, "Only U.S. citizens and Green Card holders! SIVs should come at 6:00 a.m.!" However, I noticed that they allowed people who were accompanied by women and children even if they didn't have any documents at all, much less SIV documents. While walking back to retrieve my family, I realized that someone from the crowd had stolen my wallet.

I woke my wife up and told her that we were leaving for the U.S. I asked the taxi driver to help us carry the bags to the gate and before we parted, I gave him a hundred dollars. Even if I had given him a thousand dollars, it still would not have been enough to thank him properly for his valuable assistance. It wasn't the first time I had ridden with him. His route was close to the RSM headquarters in Kabul where I had worked, and he would often drive me home or to the university where I studied for my master's degree in international relations. As we moved through the crowd, I asked the driver to follow my wife and daughter closely so they wouldn't get lost in the crowd. It took us thirty minutes to get to the crossing line. I showed my papers to the Marines. They verified the documents with our passports and then let us cross through the gate and into Kabul Airport.

Inside, there were two spots where U.S. Marines were frisking people and rifling through their belongings. At the first spot, it seemed that they were looking for bombs. They opened bags and simply moved their hands around inside to feel for any solid objects. At the second spot, they did a much more concentrated search. They emptied each bag on the ground and properly checked every item. There were two very long lines at the second spot—one for men, and one for women. There were far more men; our line was so long that I couldn't see my wife and daughter as they passed through the security check.

I spent three hours in that line. Meanwhile, I wanted to call my dad to let him know about our recent change of plans. I didn't want him or my brother to bring me the power bank early the next morning only to find out we weren't outside the gate. But, because of the jammers inside the airport, I couldn't get any signal on my phone. It turned out that only one company's SIM cards, Etisalat, worked. Luckily, there were very few people who had Etisalat SIM cards. I asked one man if I could use his phone and let my father know that we had made it through the gate. He gave me his phone to make the call. My father was relieved to hear we were safe.

After passing through the security check, we waited for another thirty minutes for a bus to take us to the military section of the airport, which was a two-story building where U.S./NATO forces frequently held conferences. When I worked as a trilingual interpreter for NATO, I twice attended meetings there. Now, the building was repurposed into a makeshift terminal for evacuation efforts. Whenever the Marines allowed people to move forward, the crowd surged.

It took us almost an hour to move ten feet. Everyone was pushing and shoving and the weather was getting hotter and hotter. There wasn't enough potable water. Children were crying.

The Marines advised, "Let the women and children go and wait for you in the shade near the terminal gate. Once you have been processed, you will be able to retrieve them." I asked my wife to take our daughter and wait in the shade until I came for them. I gave her one of the two large bags and told her not to leave the area no matter what happened.

Initially, there was a five-hour delay in the process because there was no plane available. We just sat on the ground and waited. Meanwhile, the Marines brought in more wood and plastic barriers to create proper lines for people, but when the process started again, large, unruly crowds cut into the lines. It was absolute chaos, a scene I will *never* forget. Though the Marines had asked everyone to let their female family members and children go and wait for them in the shade, most people hadn't listened. I saw children being trampled on and nearly suffocated. Many parents put their kids on their shoulders to help them breathe. The children were wailing with fear and discomfort.

I still had three pieces of luggage—two backpacks and a large bag. I put the backpacks on me, one on my back and the other on my chest, and held the large bag in my hand, pushing it forward through the crowd. I also had a small bag that contained all the documents and some money. People around me were pushing very hard and I was having difficulty holding onto everything. Then, a lady noticed that I was struggling. She took my large bag and carried it for three hours. When I realized that she wouldn't make it to the front of the line with the bag, I thanked her and asked her to just leave it there.

When I finally made it to the front of the line, things were even more chaotic. The two bags I had on me were quite heavy and prevented me from either standing up or sitting down. When people pushed, I would fall, and then couldn't get up quickly. I was trampled twice and felt close to death with all the weight and pressure. A couple of times, I nearly left the line, just to get out of the crowd so I could breathe.

But when I imagined life under the Taliban, I realized it was better to suffer for a period of hours rather than for a whole lifetime. Also, by this time, I hadn't seen my wife and daughter for more than ten hours and this strengthened my resolve. I knew I just had to hang in there and keep trying.

It was only after a hundred additional Marines were sent in that the situation finally got under control. They pushed people back and asked them to gather in different spots and form into several groups so that they could be processed in a proper order. As I was finally near the front of the line, I was included in the first group. But before I presented my documents to the Marines, I informed one of them that I needed to find my family first.

"What! Why isn't your family with you?" he asked, sounding surprised. It turned out he was part of a new team and wasn't aware of the advice the other Marines had given us in the morning.

After I explained everything, he agreed to help me find my family, but there was yet another snag. The spot I had shown my wife to stay at was now part of the area that the Marines had cordoned off to push the crowds back. They had established a new boundary line about seventy yards from the terminal gate. The Marine accompanied me, and I reunited with my family, but only after thirteen hours had passed.

Shazia later told me that after several hours of being separated from me, she had become very worried. At one point, she had asked one of the Marines—through an interpreter—to call my name on the loudspeakers so she could make sure I was okay, but because of all the shouting and crying and pushing, I hadn't heard my name. When I didn't answer, Shazia had started crying, thinking that something bad must have happened to me. The Marine then promised her that he would connect her to me no matter what happened.

In the very same hall where I had provided interpretation at two very high level security conferences while working for NATO as a linguist, now U.S. Marines were processing people for flights out of Kabul. They scanned our passports, took our fingerprints, and put white wristbands on our arms. I asked one of them about our destination.

"You will first go to Qatar and stay there for a night or two. Then you will be taken to the U.S.," he replied.

Then, they guided us to one of the aircraft hangars close by to wait for our flight. We were given water and Meals Ready to Eat (MRE), food given to soldiers in times of conflict and/or training. I asked Shazia to try and sleep and put our daughter next to her lap so she could also sleep. They slept for only two hours on the floor. I couldn't sleep, as I was very worried about losing our belongings if I dosed off. At 4:00 a.m., we were told to prepare for departure, and I woke my wife and daughter up. We walked to an area behind the terminal. There, the U.S. Marines scanned our wristbands and cleared us for the flight. We were part of the first group to get on a C-17. I had seen images of C-17s evacuating people from Kabul airport in previous days, and I knew there might be as many as 450 Afghan refugees on the flight.

The U.S. Air Force captain on the plane asked me to translate for him and his men and to assist with seating passengers correctly on the plane. He explained, "The seats on the two sides of the plane are for the elderly, women with babies on their laps, and pregnant women. Others should sit on the floor so we can accommodate as many people as possible."

This wasn't an easy task. Everyone was tired and frustrated. Those who got on first grabbed the seats, even if they were not among the three categories the captain had specified. I convinced over a hundred people to give up their seats to the elderly, women with babies, and pregnant women. A few of them resisted despite all the explanations I provided.

I advised the captain to get a bit harsh, saying, "Tell them to leave their seats and sit on the floor or they will be sent back. They won't listen to me." It worked. No one wanted to risk being ousted from the flight.

The destination for the three-and-a-half-hour flight was a U.S. Air Force base in Qatar. As the plane took off, people started quieting down and closing their eyes to go to sleep. Everyone was absolutely exhausted. I, however, couldn't sleep despite the fact that I hadn't slept for over thirty-six hours.

First, because I was very happy that we had finally departed, and second, because I couldn't stop ruminating on what had happened to my country and people. The more the plane cleared Afghanistan's airspace, the more I felt as if I was losing something irreplaceable. Memories of the good days of the past twenty years were flooding my mind. In spite of seeing Taliban militants on the streets of Kabul the day before and being on a plane to Qatar, I still thought that it might have all been a dream and that I might soon wake up and see that everything was as it was before. But it wasn't a dream. This was the new reality—for me and my family—and for my people and my country.

CHAPTER SIX
PROBLEMS IN QATAR AND GERMANY

August 20, 2021: Under a US Air Force C-17 cargo plane on the tarmac of US Air Force base Al-Udeid, Doha, Qatar.

It was 7:30 a.m. local time in Qatar when we landed at Al Udeid Air Base, which was primarily operated by Qatar Air Force and the U.S. Air Force. The temperature was 35°C, quite warm for that part of the day in comparison to Kabul's weather. We were told that since other planes had arrived earlier and their passengers needed to be unloaded first, we would have to wait for a couple of hours before de-planing. By this time, I had become the unofficial interpreter between the C-17 plane crew and my fellow Afghans. I was used to this—I often employed my experience to help solve problems whenever and wherever they arose. For instance, at one point I asked all the male passengers to avoid using the restroom for an hour until the women and girls had their opportunity. Because I was among the first group that boarded the plane and had been translating for the crew, I probably seemed more like a U.S. citizen working for the military in the evacuation process than an ordinary Afghan escaping for his life like everyone else.

Although the plane had four air conditioners running at full speed, the temperature inside was still very warm. The evacuees asked the captain to open the plane doors so we could breathe some fresh air. But he declined the request, saying, "I'm sorry, but in the last few days, after a few planes opened the doors, some people ran away and scattered around the base. Qatari personnel had to chase them down and get them back on the proper planes." But after a couple of hours, he realized that the conditions were unbearable. He opened the side door and lowered the back door of the plane, but it still wasn't cool enough.

The passengers promised to remain near the plane if they were allowed to stretch and get some fresh air. By this time, nearly four hours had passed and the captain realized that the passengers couldn't take any more of the heat. He took pity on us and allowed us to deplane for a while to cool off. However, after two more hours there was still no sign of any buses to get us to the evacuee sites. Now mid-afternoon, the weather was even hotter outside than it was inside the plane. About half of the passengers, my wife and daughter included, did not get off at all. They stayed inside to recharge their mobile phones, hoping to contact family and friends.

There was no food, and water was in short supply. I noticed some U.S. personnel on the ground and I asked the captain to ask them for any food or drink they could spare.

We were only able to obtain around twenty packages of MREs, so I handed out one package to be shared by several families and emphasized that they were for the kids. They gave us some water as well, but it was from pallets that had been sitting out in the sun. The bottles were so hot that you almost couldn't touch them.

Another problem was the C-17 restroom. It wasn't built for use by so many people and given the physical stress we'd all endured at Kabul airport, many needed to use it twice, if not multiple times, during the ten-plus hours since we had left Kabul. It finally became clogged, causing passengers who needed to relieve themselves to go out onto the sand and open space to do so. While this wasn't a problem for the men, it was a humiliating ordeal for the women. Each woman needed four others to hold their scarfs together to offer privacy, but the wind in the airfield made even that extremely difficult.

By 2:00 p.m., passengers were passing out from the heat and exhaustion. On average, every thirty minutes or so, someone would faint, and an ambulance would rush to the plane. Among those who passed out was a soldier from one of the Zero units. After an ambulance took him away, his wife and children started crying. Having witnessed all the chaos at Kabul Airport, she was afraid she might not reconnect with her husband. I assured her that nothing like that would happen, that I had worked for over eight years with the Coalition Forces and understood military procedures. I promised her that if any problem arose, I would speak to the authorities and retrieve her husband.

At one point, I felt that I was about to pass out too. That was a wake-up call. I knew I had to remain hydrated enough to get my family through this ordeal safely. I spoke with the

U.S. personnel on the ground who had some refrigerated water in the back of a pickup truck. They gave me one bottle and the captain slipped me a protein bar, which helped a lot.

At 4:00 p.m., we learned that some buses were about to arrive to take us to a hangar somewhere on the base. Things got unruly quickly as everyone wanted to be the first to get on the buses. I heard one of the U.S. military personnel on the ground shout that we needed to stay calm, and that we were all going to the same place. Still, the passengers wouldn't calm down, so I stood up and said I would translate what they were saying.

I explained to them in Dari and Pashto, "Look! Here is the plan. There will be ten buses, and since we are all going to the same area, women and children will be sent first because they are the most vulnerable, and then the men will take the following buses. Is everyone okay with this? If you agree, raise your hand!" It was the best solution I could think of at that moment, and everyone agreed to it. When I told the U.S. military about it, they were very pleased.

Finally, the buses arrived, and the U.S. military began escorting evacuees and loading them on board. I sent my wife and daughter on the last bus for the women, and because I needed to stay back and translate if there were any issues, I was the last person on the last bus. We traveled across the base to a large hangar which accommodated about two thousand people and was divided into five sections separated by pallet barriers and fold-up military beds. There was a long line where U.S. personnel were handing out food packages, hygiene items, and clothes, and I noticed that some people were trying to cut ahead.

I scolded them authoritatively in Dari and Pashto, "This is not Afghanistan. Everyone deserves to be treated equally, so please respect the line. We will all get through and get what we need." Then, an officer asked me to move behind the counter and help them hand out the items to the evacuees as it made the distribution easier and quicker (because no translation was needed in this case). Though I was extremely tired and really needed sleep, I agreed. I have always enjoyed helping others.

After about an hour, around ten men from my flight approached me. "Hey you! Come here! We need to talk!" they said angrily. I told them that I was busy and that I would see them later, but they insisted. "Our families are lost," they complained. "You are responsible for all of this, and now you need to find them!" After I asked a U.S. military officer what was going on, she said one of the buses that carried the women and children was missing and that they might have been taken to another hangar.

I told the irate men, "Look! It is not my fault. The Americans said that we were all going to the same place and you all agreed to send the women and children first. I tried to help. That's it. Please go and ask the Americans where your families are." I asked the officer to please help them and left to be with my family and hopefully find a relatively comfortable place to rest. It had been nearly seventy-two hours since I hadn't gotten any sleep.

I woke up after sleeping for only two hours. I felt pain all over my body. I was too tired to sleep. Everyone else was asleep though, so I grabbed my phone and went to find a Wi-Fi signal. I got in touch with my family back in Afghanistan and my brothers in the U.S. I texted them that we were safe and in Qatar. I did not have any information about our next destination, but I assured my family not to worry about us. I kept following the news on social media.

Videos and images of people around Kabul Airport were on everyone's page. I also realized that the U.S. Marines at the airport gates were now applying stricter rules regarding who to allow inside. I breathed a heavy sigh of relief knowing that we had made it through in the nick of time.

As hours passed, the people surrounding me began waking up, and after talking to a few of them, I realized that my voice was hoarse. I could hardly say a word. It felt so painful when I talked. Then, a U.S. military officer told me, "Start waking everyone up in your area. Your flight is at 7:00 a.m. You are going to Germany."

With my extreme sore throat and the fact that I knew I would be blamed again if something else went wrong, I didn't want to translate on the second leg of the journey. But one of my fellow Afghans insisted, "It is you or no one. You don't need to do everything. I will be your partner. You just tell me what needs to be done, and I will make sure it happens." But when the time came to corral people into lines, he was nowhere to be found.

As soon as we lined up, around a hundred people—evacuees from other groups—started cutting in line and joining our group. Though there was a first-to-arrive, first-to-go procedure, the evacuees were afraid that they would be left behind and they were panicking.

I told the U.S. soldiers, "They won't stop if you are nice to them. You can't fit all these people on a single plane. I know who was on our flight from Kabul. I will point out those who are not supposed to be on our flight. Don't listen to them and don't allow them on board under any circumstances." Then, to make my movement easier, I asked two gentlemen who were on their own for help with our luggage. "Please carry them on the plane. I will get them back from you once I get on board." Thankfully, they agreed to help and look after my bags.

When they removed the interlopers, the line finally began to move, but when I got on board a C-17 again, I didn't see anyone from the first half of our group, including the two gentlemen carrying my bags. When I asked a soldier about them, he told me they had left on an earlier flight. Shazia and I were very upset. I slumped down to the floor. I had a very bad sore throat and I simply didn't have the energy to help my fellow Afghans or the plane crew any longer. As my wife and daughter had slept reasonably well at the hangar in Qatar, I gave Shazia the small bag with our documents and money and told her to stay awake so we wouldn't lose anything else. Then, I laid down and finally fell asleep. It was a six-hour flight from Qatar to Germany.

At around 4 p.m. on August 21, 2021, we landed at the U.S. Air Force Base Ramstein, Germany. The area around the base was very beautiful and we received a warm welcome by the U.S. and German military personnel. Little did we know that we would be staying there for over a week!

First, we were tested for Covid-19, which took almost an hour. Then, we were guided to a hall from where we would later move into different rooms for in-processing and biometric registration. The hall had two sections; one was designated for those who had landed earlier, and the other for those who arrived later. As the evacuees in the first section moved forward, people from the second section moved to the first one. Volunteers from the United Service Organization (USO) provided water and snacks as well as crayons and paper to keep the kids entertained.

When we entered the hall, I saw around one hundred personnel from the Zero units and their families from a previous flight still waiting to get out of the first section and into the in-processing rooms. About a half hour later, I noticed that several dozen people from our flight were also pushing hard to get into the biometric registration rooms. Things were getting unruly again. The Zero units personnel wouldn't allow those from our flight into their section and those who arrived later were refusing to comply and wait for their turn. I was so fed up with the chaos along the journey that I didn't want to be involved in any part of the official process any longer. Some U.S. personnel shut the doors and a U.S. captain warned, "Please be quiet and go back. Please respect the line. Unless you do that, we will not open the doors."

When I listened to the interpretation, I realized that the interpreter—a lady in her fifties from Pakistan—was translating from English into Urdu, the language of the people in Pakistan. There were several problems with this. First, Urdu wasn't the language that all of the evacuees understood. Only a small number of Afghans in eastern Afghanistan and in Kabul understood it, because of spending years as refugees in Pakistan during the civil war in Afghanistan and because of watching Indian movies which are in Hindi language that is quite similar to Pakistan's Urdu. Therefore, she needed to be translating into Dari and/or Pashto, the two common languages of Afghanistan.

In addition, she didn't respect the principle of first-arrived, first-processed. Instead, she allowed the elderly, allegedly out of respect for them, to move to the in-processing rooms before those who had arrived first and were still waiting in lines. The problem in this case was that the elderly folks weren't alone; most were accompanied by a family of up to ten people. I realized that if someone didn't step in to resolve the confusion, we would also be waiting for hours. I decided to tell the captain what the problem was. I recommended that they remove the interpreter and bring in another one who could speak Dari and Pashto, or at least one of the two languages. I said, "I know it may take some time, so I will cover for her until a new interpreter arrives." It turned out to be four long hours, and another interpreter never arrived.

At about 10:00 p.m., it was finally time for me and my family. The U.S. biometric personnel fingerprinted us, made copies of our passports and Afghan ID cards, and we were then taken to the camp. On the way in, we were given hygiene items and provided dinner by the American Red Cross and U.S. personnel. The camp consisted of around eighty makeshift tents and a huge hangar, and each tent had twenty or so fold-up military beds. The tents were for the men and the hangar was for the women and children. The power to the tents was provided by generators.

One of the tents was the command post of the U.S. Military and had a Wi-Fi signal. I texted my family in Kabul and my brothers in the U.S. to let them know we had made it to Germany, but didn't know when we would leave and where we would be taken next. Then, I took off my shoes after nearly five days with minimal sleep and crawled into bed to finally get some much-needed rest.

The first thing I did the following morning was to search for the two gentlemen who had my bags. Thankfully, one of the evacuees who recognized me said, "They are in tent number eight. They have been looking for you." I was so relieved. I found the men who had helped me, got the bags, and took them to my tent. After that, I went for breakfast, but there was a *very* long line and the weather was cold.

Luckily, I had saved some snacks from the previous night and that was enough to tide me over. Then, I went to get in touch with Shazia, but I couldn't get a Wi-Fi signal after hundreds of evacuees had gathered around the U.S. military command post tent. That entire day, I didn't see or even speak with my wife and daughter. There was simply no way to communicate with them.

The makeshift camp at Ramstein Air Force Base had been constructed quickly and recently. Everything seemed fairly new, but the camp wasn't really ready to accommodate so many people. There were portable toilets, but no showers. Many of us, myself included, hadn't showered in days, and after having been through all the chaos, scorching hot days, and ever-present dust in Kabul, Qatar, and now Germany, everyone smelled absolutely awful. We used bottled water to clean ourselves or wash our clothes, as most of us had come with only the clothes on our backs. I cleaned my body with wipes and washed my hair with bottled water. I washed my trousers and shoes, and thankfully had packed two clean shirts in one of our bags. I finally began to feel a bit human again. It is worth noting that the U.S. military later distributed clothes and shoes to almost all the evacuees at the camp.

Another issue was food distribution. The U.S. military provided three meals to over three thousand evacuees every day. The problem was not a shortage of food, but a lack of distribution sites and personnel. There was only one meal distribution site, so actually getting food took hours. A thousand people would form the line hours before the meal was even cooked. After I found my wife and daughter during our second day at Ramstein, Shazia would stand in line and then bring me boxed meals. Lima did not eat the food at the camp, only the bread. She preferred the snacks we still had from Afghanistan and Qatar.

Coincidentally, seven male members of two families whose female members had their beds placed next to those of my wife and daughter were my tentmates. They made it easier for me and my family to call and meet each other when needed (only the kids were allowed to enter the women's hangar). After a few days, the U.S. military assigned a couple of sergeants to 24-7 duty at the gate of the hangar for women and children. They would ask the male evacuees the names of their female family members and then call them on loudspeakers.

Day three at Ramstein was Lima's second birthday, but we were in no mood to celebrate. We were lucky that she was too young to remember or understand that it was her birthday. I couldn't do anything for her, so I just kissed her, holding back my tears. I didn't want Shazia to see me so upset. I tried to convince myself that taking Lima to the U.S., where she would be safe and have a prosperous future, was the best birthday gift we could give her. Truly, one of my primary reasons for writing this book was to let her know, when she grows up, how she came to live in America.

Meanwhile, the U.S. military wanted to communicate with just a few people every day rather than having to explain things repeatedly to three thousand-plus evacuees. They asked the people in each tent to choose a representative, and I was chosen for mine. We met with the camp commander, a female U.S. Air Force colonel, at least once every day, and she updated us on what was going on. We would ask questions and recommend solutions.

A dozen volunteers from among the evacuees started helping the U.S. military with the distribution of meals, and the U.S. military brought in shower units and distributed winter clothes to the evacuees.

On day four, the camp commander announced that we would be leaving for the U.S. in a few days. The U.S. citizens and their families would go first, followed by the Green Card holders and their families. Then U.S. visa holders and their families would make up the third group out of Ramstein, and the fourth group—our group—would include everyone else. The first three categories of evacuees left the camp on August 24 and 25, 2021.

Finally, on August 26, we were told to prepare for our flight to the U.S. Initially, we were told we would be taken to a terminal and from there to a chartered plane. Everyone gathered in front of the gate and the U.S. military established various lines of control to help everyone leave the camp smoothly and in a proper order. Then, we waited outside for nearly nine hours for the buses. It became freezing cold, so I gave my blanket to my wife and daughter, and I just did my best to assess the proceedings.

At 4:00 a.m. the following morning, we were told that our plane had arrived, and we were taken to a C-17 hangar for out-processing. We were so excited to get on the plane, but then had to wait for over twenty-four hours in the hangar. First, they searched our bags. Then, the U.S. Department of Homeland Security (DHS) staff checked our documents. They returned our passports, but kept the papers we were given when we had first arrived at Ramstein. Following that, we were guided to a waiting area in the hangar.

At 2:00 p.m., a couple of U.S. military personnel returned the papers they had taken from us earlier. After an hour, they asked everyone to line up for a security background check by the DHS staff. When we approached the out-processing area, I noticed that there were four U.S. Customs and Border Protection (CBP) agents monitoring things. They were taking pictures of everyone and uploading them to their system. They separated our group into two; clearing one for the flight and asking the other to wait.

At 8:00 p.m., we were instructed to line up for another security check by CBP agents. This time, they separated twenty-seven people from the line, including me and my family. They sent us to a different waiting area while the others were cleared for the flight to the U.S. None of the other people spoke English well, so I had to make sure we could determine what was happening and end any confusion as questions arose.

Earlier, when the CBP agents were taking our pictures, I realized that our names and/or images matched those of some Arabs on the CBP database. I spoke to one of the CBP agents who assured me that though there were some security issues, we should expect to be cleared and fly out soon. We had no choice but to sit tight.

While we waited in the hangar, we were given food, but there was no place to sleep. In addition, the large gates of the hangar were kept wide open and the cold wind was blowing in, making it extremely uncomfortable for the women and children. The U.S. military tried to help by providing blankets, but there weren't enough for everyone. When I asked them to at least close the gates, they refused. Hours passed with new evacuees arriving and departing, but there was no update for us. The evacuees in our waiting area were sprawled everywhere trying to sleep, some on chairs, others on the floor. After a while, we decided to take a nap too, but just as I was falling asleep, one of the evacuees came over to me and said, "Hey, they are taking some people out."

I got up and went to see what was going on. CBP agents were taking evacuees out of the waiting area, taking their pictures, and uploading them to the system. If anyone appeared to match with a suspicious individual on the CBP database, they would be brought back to the waiting area for further scrutiny. After a while, we were called in for this part of the process and thankfully were cleared to fly.

After more than thirty hours of "detention," at 2:00 p.m. on August 28, 2021, we finally boarded a United Airlines plane. It was a large one and would be carrying over three hundred people. One of the flight attendants, an Afghan American in his fifties who also served as the interpreter, announced that there was a one-hour delay due to a technical problem. Once again, it seemed that we would never make it to our destination, but we finally flew out of U.S. Air Force Base Ramstein at 3:00 p.m. It was a seven-and-a-half-hour flight from Germany to the U.S., and it was *the* best part of our long and frustrating journey so far. We were so happy that I cannot describe the joy in words.

The plane had Wi-Fi, and we also could watch movies and TV shows. After using the Wi-Fi for an hour to get in touch with my family in Afghanistan and my brothers in the U.S., I watched *Those Who Wish Me Dead*, a 2021 Hollywood movie. It was hard not to think of those who had indeed wished me dead in Kabul, and who would continue to put my fellow Afghans at risk for the foreseeable future. But even though the Taliban were now in our rearview mirror, I knew my family still had a long way to go before I could feel we were finally safe.

CHAPTER SEVEN
TWO MONTHS AT FORT McCOY

August 31, 2021: With my family at US Army base Fort McCoy, Wisconsin, USA, where we spent 65 days.

We arrived at Dulles International Airport on August 28, 2021 at 10:00 p.m. local time. I didn't want to rush, so I chose to be the last person to exit the plane. We waited in line for three hours before the CBP agents at Dulles stamped our passports and did our biometrics. Most of the evacuees didn't have documents with them to prove their identities or Afghan government-issued passports to be stamped, and this caused confusion for the CBP agents. Additionally, more than half of the evacuees didn't speak English and the interpretation doubled the time needed to clear everyone. We were taken next to another part of the airport where we got tested for Covid, had dinner, and then waited for another hour for buses before being transported to Dulles Expo Center where a large area had been turned into a makeshift camp to host thousands of Afghan evacuees.

The center functioned as the main transit site for the distribution of evacuees to various camps across the U.S. It was a wonderful place. There were over a thousand Afghan Americans supporting the various U.S. government and nongovernment agencies working to process the evacuees. They were really helpful. More importantly, it was the first time in ten days that we had typical Afghan meals and there were proper showers. Whenever a new group of evacuees entered, all of the staff at the center gave a *standing ovation*, which gave us such a good feeling. It was the first time we actually started to believe we might be free to build a new life in America.

At around 5:00 p.m. on August 29, 2021, we were notified to get ready to board our next plane, and we lifted off at 6:00 p.m. EST time for a two-hour flight on Delta Airlines to Wisconsin. We landed at La Crosse Regional Airport and were then transported to Fort McCoy, a U.S. Army base where we were registered and then tested for Covid-19. After that, U.S. Army personnel, among them some Afghan Americans, briefed us on the rules and regulations of the base as well as our rights and responsibilities. We were given hygiene items, blankets, pillows, and bed sheets by the American Red Cross and then taken to our accommodations, two-story barracks. We settled on the first floor. There were six other families with us in the same room.

1. The Mashal Family: A family of eight including a husband and wife and six children, ages five, ten, thirteen, fifteen, seventeen, and eighteen. Mr. Mashal had worked at the

United States Institute of Peace (USIP) in Kabul. Originally from the eastern province of Nangarhar, the Mashals had an approved SIV case and had been interviewed at the U.S. Embassy in Kabul. They departed on their own from Fort McCoy two days after us. Their movement and resettlement to Colorado was sponsored by a charity organization.

2. The Momand Family: A family of five including a husband and wife, their baby boy (one year old), Mr. Momand's brother, and Mrs. Momand's brother (both in their twenties). They were originally from the eastern Nangarhar Province and recently from Kabul where Mr. Momand had worked as a finance expert in various organizations. He had recently applied for an SIV. They joined us two weeks later and departed on their own from Fort McCoy almost a month after we left. They all went to Virginia where the in-laws of Mr. Momand's brother lived.

3. The Rahimi Family: A family of two, a husband and wife, who had recently gotten married. Mr. Rahimi, in his sixties, was a U.S. citizen, but his wife, in her forties, was not. A former schoolteacher who had joined the Afghan army in the 1990s, Mr. Rahimi was originally from the northeastern Kapisa Province. They now live in Sacramento, California, where I usually visit them.

4. The Kohbandi Family: A family of four, including a husband and wife with a baby boy (two years old), and Mr. Kohbandi's brother. Originally from the northeastern Kapisa Province, they had an approved SIV case, but didn't reveal who they had worked for in Afghanistan. They left Fort McCoy more than a month after we departed. They went to live with Mr. Kohbandi's brother in Los Angeles, California.

5. The Sayed Zada Family: A family of four, including a husband and wife with two children ages four and six.

Originally from Kabul, Mr. Sayed Zada had worked for a foreign contracting company at Kabul Airport. They wanted to go to Virginia where one of Mr. Sayed Zada's closest friends lived and could offer employment at his restaurant. They chose to remain at Fort McCoy until they were taken to Arizona on January 13, 2022, through the normal resettlement process. (They relocated to Virginia after only one month in Arizona!)

6. The Shinwari Family: A family of two, a husband and wife. The wife, a U.S. citizen in her fifties, had recently married a handsome young Afghan man in his thirties. The wife went to Georgia in mid-October after her son died, and the husband left through the normal resettlement process a week before we left.

The barracks at Fort McCoy had central heating and showers with hot and cold water. There were a few specific areas with Wi-Fi signals, we could shop at the on-base store, and there were multiple areas called "grab-and-go" where U.S. Army personnel handed out snacks and drinks 24-7. The U.S. Army soldiers held movie nights for men, women, and children, and handed out footballs and volleyballs so the kids could play and burn off steam. There were multiple laundry facilities on the base where we could wash our clothes for free. They also had a post office, so we were able to receive mail promptly from our friends and families who lived across the U.S.

Lack of adequate and timely medical services was really the biggest issue we faced at Fort McCoy, which only had one small health clinic for the thirteen thousand-plus evacuees. Even though it operated 24-7, it was a pretty small center, and the usual waiting time was around four hours. Only a few doctors and around fifteen nurses worked at the clinic, and medication was always in short supply. In addition, the procedures the clinic employed were unfamiliar to a great number of us, which added to the confusion. In order to avoid a shortage of medication, a private company was hired to deliver necessary medication for the evacuees at their buildings. According to the U.S. Army, the medication should have been delivered within a window of seventy-two hours, but many received their medicine well after they had already recovered from their ailments.

Most of the Afghan evacuees entered the U.S. through Dulles International Airport. Our luggage, however, was not returned to us immediately upon arrival; we were told that our belongings would be delivered to our final destination. Many of these bags contained cash, jewelry, and documents, while others were packed with clothes. Before the resettlement process began at Fort McCoy, the search for our bags was a daily concern. Mr. Mashal, Mr. Rahimi, Mr. Kohbandi, Mr. Shinwari, and I would walk for hours every day from one block to another across the base, looking for our belongings. After authorities realized that separating the evacuees from their luggage was not a wise move, they started bringing in the bags and the evacuees at the same time.

But there were still problems, such as the fact that when the U.S. Army dropped the bags onto the street, there was no one to watch over them. After some evacuees realized that soldiers of the Afghan Zero units had huge amounts of cash (U.S. dollars) in their bags, they started looking to remove and rifle through any military-style bags (the Zero units were given large amounts of cash money when leaving Kabul to compensate for their months-long pending salaries, as well as severance and a bonus for their years of service). Jewelry was another incentive for some to steal.

Most Afghan women are given huge amounts of gold in the form of necklaces, bracelets, bangles, rings, and earrings. Some of them, in a hurry to get to Kabul airport, hadn't worn their jewelry, but instead had put it in their luggage.

Many evacuees had put their important documents — passports, ID cards, and SIV papers — in their bags, and they needed those documents to identify themselves to authorities during the resettlement process. Additionally, most of us had arrived with only the clothes we were wearing; the only extra clothes many of us had were those handed out on the planes from Germany to the U.S. Those who hadn't been to Germany before coming to the U.S. lacked even those extras pieces of clothing.

Finally, in late September we heard some informative news — all of our bags were in a warehouse in Landover, Maryland. We were told that in order to affect the timely evacuation from Germany, Qatar, and elsewhere under such fraught conditions, they had decided to concentrate solely on getting as many passengers as possible on the flights and would then get the luggage to the eventual locations separately. I also heard that due to the chaos, the bags hadn't been properly searched at Kabul airport, so the DHS would be conducting a thorough search later before anything would be released. We were asked to submit online forms to claim our bags. It seemed to us that the problem was more than the government on its own could handle, and we were relieved when a private company, EMS, was hired to sort out the luggage and deliver it to evacuees at various places throughout the U.S.

We had three bags. I found two of them on the portal and they were delivered to us on December 9, 2021 (over a hundred days after they were separated from us). Four days later, the EMS called me and said that they had found my third bag and that it would be delivered to me shortly. It was supposed to arrive on December 21, 2021, by no later than 1:15 p.m., but less than thirty minutes before it was delivered to me, the delivery services were contacted by the EMS and instructed to return the bag. When I inquired about the delay with the EMS, I was told that someone else had claimed to own the bag and that once the dispute was resolved, it would be shipped to me. I finally received it on January 19, 2022, nearly six months after it was separated from us!

After more than a month at Fort McCoy, the male evacuees really needed haircuts. There was a barbershop in a store on the base, but it was only for the U.S. military personnel. Fortunately, there was a barber among our group of evacuees (though he was not a barber by profession). He worked with a small hair and beard trimmer, a paper scissor, a comb, and a spray bottle. By the end of our second month at Fort McCoy, there were several professional barbers (among the Afghan evacuees) available to us, and that really helped bring a sense of normalcy to hundreds of us. Once I asked one of them about his journey, he said, "I never worked with foreigners. My house and shop were right across from the airport, and when I saw that everyone was rushing into the airport, I took my family too to give it a try, and here I am."

When we arrived at Fort McCoy, an Afghan American U.S. Army sergeant said, "You will be here for a maximum of two weeks. Then, you will be taken to the states of your choice." But as our stay at the camp became prolonged, the U.S. Army at Fort McCoy began holding weekly meetings with representatives of the evacuees. U.S. Army Captain

Figueroa, in charge of blocks twenty-seven and twenty-eight, required two guests (the term was used to refer to all the evacuees out of respect for them) from each building to attend, and my roommates asked me to represent them. Initially, the meetings were focused on resolving issues pertaining to the well-being of the guests—security, safety, accommodations, DFACs, health services, laundry services, sexual harassment complaints, domestic violence issues, etc. Later, when the different phases of the resettlement process began, updates about each phase and various protocols were shared and discussed with the representatives.

Captain Figueroa was a very effective leader who would listen patiently to the representatives and then do his best to resolve any problems and accurately answer all questions. Soon, representatives of the U.S. Chamber of Commerce offered presentations to the guests on all employment-related topics. The International Rescue Committee (IRC) was also involved in the resettlement process and had multiple offices on the base. The U.S. Army and the IRC had their own Afghan American interpreters who spoke both Dari and Pashto pretty well, but the U.S. Chamber of Commerce representatives needed a Pashto-speaking interpreter. As there was no one more capable, I offered to help.

Initially, the U.S. Army at Fort McCoy used less than ten Afghan Americans who served in the U.S. Amry as interpreters, but it was soon obvious that it wasn't enough. As the U.S. government agencies involved in the evacuation and resettlement processes hadn't yet hired civilian interpreters, around a hundred evacuees who spoke English assumed the role, most voluntarily, and others were pressed to help by the U.S. Department of State. They were assigned to the DFACs, the clothes distribution warehouse, and community centers that handed out baby formula and hygiene items. Though at the end of each day, the U.S. Army gave them full bags, many volunteers kept the better items for themselves, their families, and friends, which caused anger among other guests. After the U.S. government-hired interpreters arrived and replaced the volunteers, these problems were resolved.

Also, the fire alarms at some of the buildings went off multiple times every day, and this soon became a jarring, semi-frequent occurrence. The U.S. Army had advised the guests upon arrival at the base to look after their children and prevent them from setting off the alarms, but that was easier said than done. One reason was that the alarms were placed pretty low on the walls and easily reached by kids. Also, the alarms had a bright red color, and therefore the little kids thought they were toys. But worst of all, some adults tripped the alarms by smoking cigarettes in the toilets. Anytime someone set off an alarm, the sirens of fire trucks, ambulances and Military Police (MP) patrol cars would be heard everywhere across the camp as they raced in to deal with the situation.

Among the guests at Fort McCoy were more than two hundred university students (all girls) who had attended the Asian University for Women (AUW). They were residing together in the largest buildings on the base, and some began teaching English to other guests at the camp. They and some other women and girls started dressing up in what was deemed by some male guests as anti-Islamic and against Afghan culture and tradition. The girls were criticized, harassed, and even threatened. At one point, I observed a U.S. Army sergeant escorting two of the girls any time they went to the DFAC.

The issue prompted Fort McCoy's gender advisor, a female U.S. Army major, to attend the weekly meetings with the representatives, and later, multiple cultural and legal awareness sessions were organized for male and female guests, separately. The sessions also covered legal matters pertaining to the protection of children. This issue was raised because many of the guest parents at Fort McCoy weren't looking after their kids properly. The children played with whatever they found and were out on the streets unguarded by their parents as late as 10:00 p.m. Even, I once saw a young man taking his two small children to the store in a yellow, wheeled mop bucket.

To make matters worse, the guests who hadn't worked with foreigners back in Afghanistan weren't used to putting garbage into trash cans, much less picking up after themselves. Most of it was produced by kids sent by their parents for meals at the DFAC. Sometimes, the load was too heavy for them to carry, and they would fall and scatter food on the ground. Then there were the guests who smoked and flicked their cigarette butts on the ground. Though a private company was initially contracted to clean the washrooms twice a day and remove the garbage around the buildings, it wasn't enough. Even worse, the guests often flushed diapers, wipes, and paper towels down the toilets, which caused a huge headache for the rest of us, as well as for the base maintenance department. If the toilets on the second floor were clogged, sewage water would leak down from the ceiling of the first floor washroom, making it impossible for guests on the first floor to use the washroom.

For me, a big problem was that my daughter did not eat the food served at Fort McCoy, and Shazia and I were afraid that she might become malnourished. Also, as the weather in Wisconsin got colder, families rarely allowed the kids to play outside, and the longer they were kept indoors, more fighting among them resulted. These issues, and the following conversation I had with a United States Citizenship and Immigration Services (USCIS) staff member at the guest services office (where representatives of all relevant agencies answered questions pertaining to the entire resettlement process), led to our decision to leave on our own.

Me: How much longer will we be here?

USCIS: It could be months.

Me: Does months means we will be here for ten to twelve months?

USICS: All I can say is that it could be months.

Me: If we stay as long as it takes, will we be sent to the state of our choice?

USCIS: I cannot guarantee that.

Me: If we stay as long as it takes and finally we are told to go to another state rather than the one we have chosen, will we have the right to deny it?

USCIS: No. We will make you go there.

CHAPTER EIGHT
RESTTLEMENT

November 3, 2021: Farewell to my roommates before
leaving Fort McCoy, Wisconsin for California.

The resettlement process was initially comprised of five stages: medical examinations, forwarding address confirmation, resettlement by the International Organization for Migration (IOM), and interviews with the IRC and USCIS. Each stage took place block-by-block and building-by-building, and each occurred more than a week after the one prior. The medical examination had two parts conducted more or less simultaneously: the blood test, and the prescriptions/applications for various vaccines. But as viruses started spreading across the camp and evacuees began leaving on their own, authorities decided to first administer all the vaccines and then do the blood tests.

The interview with USCIS was for the purpose of completing Form I-765, the Application for Employment Authorization. All Afghan evacuees, SIV applicants included, were issued "parolee" status. In order for them to legally work in the U.S., they needed to apply for Employment Authorization Cards (EACs). As each individual's case was processed separately, the applications of my wife and daughter were approved quickly while mine took over a month.

The purpose of the interview with the IRC was to gather information on each guest/family's status and determine where in the U.S. they wanted to resettle. At first, we were told that if we had any immediate family members, relatives, or friends in America, we would probably be able to join them wherever they were. But it later changed.

As soon as the guests completed their medical exams, their chosen family members, relatives, or friends across the U.S. were contacted. The purpose was to ensure that the guests could be accommodated by them before the IRC and other relevant agencies involved in the resettlement process across America could find them homes and sponsors.

Once family members, relatives, or friends of guests confirmed they would house the guests for a while, the IOM would begin the out-processing stage. The guests were notified forty-eight hours before their flight. The IOM provided the tickets to anywhere across the U.S., and the first flight out took place on October 11, 2021. Initially, the IOM and the IRC worked together, with the former handling departures and the latter dealing with resettlement. After the number of guests leaving on their own increased significantly, the IOM took responsibility for the entire process while the IRC was reassigned to assist those that wanted to leave on their own.

Before the start of the mass evacuation from Afghanistan, more commonly known as Operation Allies Refuge (OAR) which later became Operations Allies Welcome (OAW), most Afghans—particularly those who had moved to the U.S. since 2010 when the SIV process first started—lived in just few specific states: California, Virginia, Texas, and Colorado. As the resettlement process ramped up, rumors spread across Fort McCoy that guests who had chosen these states would not be sent there, but instead would be sent to other states indiscriminately. It would have been very difficult in this case for the guests to start new lives where they knew no one. On the other hand, the USCIS and the IRC insisted that they didn't have enough case workers in these four states and did not have any sponsors available due to the high number of evacuees that were already there. Fort McCoy was the largest camp across America, but it wasn't the only one.

Despite the fact that the evacuees at Fort McCoy made it clear to the USCIS and the IRC that their family members, relatives, and friends would help them find houses and deal with post-resettlement issues, the two agencies still would not guarantee they would be sent to their chosen states. I would estimate that half of the guests at Fort McCoy were not taken to their states of choice. With this development, the number of those who chose to leave on their own increased significantly. The USCIS and the IRC warned the guests that if they chose to leave on their own, they might end up losing some of their benefits as well as falling back to the end of the lists for various other post-resettlement processes.

My former boss and some other friends in the U.S. insisted that we should leave the camp ASAP. One of the issues that concerned us was the fact that some guests had caused trouble—from domestic violence to sexual harassment—both before and after they were resettled across the U.S. We were afraid that if these incidents continued, the U.S. government might decide to hold up or even halt the process until the backgrounds of all evacuees were extensively examined. On October 15, 2021, I talked with my two brothers in California about our options. One of them went to check with the IRC's local office in Oakland. He was told that they would take our case as a walk-in, but that we might lose some of our benefits.

On October 19, 2021, I checked with representatives of all the agencies involved in the resettlement process and I was told that we could not leave the camp unless three weeks had passed of our blood tests. The procedure for guests leaving on their own included booking tickets, booking a taxi (the airport was forty miles from Fort McCoy), presenting copies of tickets to the IRC, attending a pre-departure briefing by the IRC, and preparing for departure. My brother booked us tickets for November 3 and arranged for a taxi service to pick us up from Fort McCoy. We set about taking care of all the preparations. The next few days were really hectic, and the anticipation of finally reaching our destination was very emotional for us.

On October 30, I went to see the IRC representatives and showed them our tickets. They made an appointment for us for November 1 with the IRC main office on the base. At that meeting, the IRC briefed us on what the likely consequences of leaving on our own were. The IRC, however, said that they could not retrieve the medical reports through their database and that we had to check with them again in the following days. The most important documents we needed before the departure were the medical reports. Therefore, we had two options: wait for the medical reports which could take more than a week, or leave without them and re-take the medical examinations (on our own cost) if the reports were required at any time or any place along our journey to California. Fortunately, they retrieved and gave us the reports the following day. Whew!

And so, at 12:45 p.m. on November 3, 2021, after spending sixty-five days at the camp, we left Fort McCoy. Though my daughter cried a lot during the thirty-minute trip from Fort McCoy to La Crosse airport because she was not used to sitting in a child's car seat, Shazia and I felt so relieved to finally be on our way to a new life. At 6:00 p.m., we lifted off with American Airlines, en route from Wisconsin to Chicago, and at 9:00 p.m. we departed Chicago for San Francisco, California. We landed at 11:30 p.m. local time. My older brother was there to meet us at the airport, and an hour later we arrived at his home in Concord, California. It had been *seventy-eight days* since we had left Kabul, Afghanistan.

The day after we settled in, I called the Social Security Administration (SSA) office to obtain Social Security Numbers (SSNs) for my family. I needed the SSN to apply for a driver's license, among other things. The SSA agent asked for my I-94 number. This is the form that the CBP generates online for anyone who visits the U.S. for the first time, but I did not have it. "I can't help you. Call back when you have your I-94 number," the agent said.

The IRC's legal office at Fort McCoy had said that SIV applicants whose cases had been approved but had not passed the interview in the U.S. Embassy in Kabul, only needed to fill out the I-485 forms to adjust their status and apply for Green Cards. But to fill out the I-485 form, I needed the number of the I-94 form. Accordingly, when we were at Fort McCoy, I had tried to obtain the I-94 forms, but was not able to.

Also, in January 2022 I applied on Miry's List, an online site dedicated to welcoming newly arrived refugee families in the U.S. and helping them turn their sparsely furnished (or unfurnished) houses into well-equipped homes. Miry's List was helping an average of thirty families each month and I was hoping they could help us as well. But my application was not approved because I did not have I-94s for my family to prove that we had resettled in the U.S. after the collapse of the Afghan government in mid-August 2021.

I tried multiple ways to get the forms. When I filled out an online inquiry form with the CBP, an auto reply email asked me for all relevant information and documents, as well as how I had previously attempted to obtain the I-94s. After providing all required information and documents, I was told that the CBP had not generated any I-94s for my family at all and that I had to either go to the original point of entry (Dulles International Airport) or visit one of the CBP's Deferred Inspection Sites in person.

In the meantime, I emailed the guest services office at Fort McCoy to see if they could retrieve the I-94s for my family and email them to me. I got the same response; the CBP had not yet generated I-94s for my family. Then, I emailed the CBP Deferred Inspection Site in San Francisco and a week later, I got a call and was told that our I-94s had been generated. But though I was able to retrieve the forms for myself and my daughter, I couldn't access the one for my wife. I sent another email to the CBP office and begged them to generate the I-94 for Shazia. Finally, after more than three months of failed attempts, I had I-94s for my entire family.

However, when I again called the SSA office about the SSNs, this time they scheduled an appointment for us, and surprisingly did not ask for the I-94 numbers at all. Also, at the second attempt, Miry's List approved my application (because I included the I-94s) and provided us with pretty much everything we immediately needed to begin life with in our new apartment.

On November 8, after we had resettled in Concord, California, I emailed the IRC to let them know about my status and start processing my case, but the IRC said that they would not accept my case as a walk-in. It seemed that between October 15 when my brother had asked the IRC whether they accepted walk-in cases and November 8, there had been some changes in their operations. I was told to wait. I again emailed the IRC on December 2, 2021, and though they responded by phone this time, the answer was the same: "Due to the high number of assigned cases, the IRC cannot accept new walk-ins."

Meanwhile, I contacted two other resettlement agencies to see if they could take my case: Jewish Family & Community Services East Bay and World Relief Sacramento. The former said that they did not have the funds to take on my case but would keep my name on file, while the latter simply said that my case had not been assigned to them and that was it.

Jewish Family & Community Services East Bay called me on January 13 and said that they had included my case on their list, but there was no guarantee that I would receive support no matter how long I waited. Instead, they offered to remove my name if I accepted a small amount of cash

(Welcome Money) plus health checkup services. I agreed to the offer. I was about to rent an apartment and needed money for it. (But, almost a year later at the time of this book's creation, I still haven't received this assistance!)

Since my case was officially assigned to the IRC, I followed up on it on January 4, 2022. The reply stated that they had put my case on the list, but there were forty-two other cases ahead of mine, and mine wouldn't be approved until the end of January 2022. The IRC should have processed these three parts of my case, if not all: providing welcome money, finding a house, and applying for Green Cards on my family's behalf. However, it only provided the welcome money and that was it. But luckily, my brother was able to rent us an apartment in his name, and most importantly, World Relief Sacramento accepted my application for adjustment of status and applied for Green Cards for my family on May 2, 2022. To properly thank the agent that processed my application for Green Cards (the paperwork took more than a month), I promised to send her a copy of this book when it got published.

Due to the governmental delays and the endless red tape, I couldn't be employed quickly. And because the resettlement agencies hadn't yet processed my case, we stayed for four-and-a-half months at the houses of my two brothers. The eldest lived in Sacramento, California, while the younger one lives in Concord (the eldest has also now moved to Concord). Shazia and I wholeheartedly *thank* them and their families for their tolerance during the time we spent at their homes, and for their assistance regarding all issues pertaining to our resettlement. Beginning a new life in the U.S. would have been impossible without their kindness and support.

I remember when the visa interview for my family was scheduled at the American Embassy in Kabul, I was so excited about moving to the U.S. My brothers, who had already relocated to California, and other friends who lived across the U.S. would tell us about the warm welcome and the huge amount of respect they had received from Americans. However, with the collapse of the Afghan government, everything changed. Fleeing from Afghanistan to the U.S. became a journey of life and death. Even after my family finally resettled in California, it didn't give us a feeling of true happiness because we'd been through so many troubles along the way and are still facing significant challenges to survive in our new country. But the cleaner air, employment opportunities, job security, better schools for the kids, 24-7 power and internet access, better roads and more made America a preferred place to live compared to Afghanistan.

At first, some things were a bit jarring and took some time getting used to. From a cultural perspective, there are major differences between America and Afghanistan. For instance, many Americans have pets like dogs and cats, while Afghans don't. For Americans, Halal meat is considered any meat not prohibited by Islam while for Muslims (and therefore most Afghans), Halal meat is that which adheres to Islamic law.

American families tend to be much smaller than Afghan ones. Renting a home in America requires several years of previous residency and proof that one earns triple the amount of the of rent. In Afghanistan, none of these are required. In addition, health, car, business, and rental insurance are common in America, but are rarely required in Afghanistan. Americans use debit and credit cards while Afghans use cash.

Despite any of that, I'm grateful to be in the U.S. But no matter how good my life might be in the future, it won't change the fact that I have lost my home country, and my people's achievements of the past twenty years are also now gone. My mother died in 2020 due to Covid-19, but the grief of losing my motherland is perhaps even more acute because it still poses such danger to so many loved ones. I left behind my father, a sister, a brother, and a sister-in-law. Though they attempted once to get into Kabul airport during the August 2021 evacuation, they didn't make it through. They were afraid of being trampled or separated from each other among the thousands of people at the airport gates.

For the time being, the Taliban have declared an overall amnesty for those who either worked with foreigners or the Afghan government, but such a promise is always tentative with the Taliban and could change at any moment. If the Taliban decide to go after families of those who worked for foreigners, they surely can find plenty of reasons and probably evidence as well to threaten, blackmail, kidnap, or kill those still in Afghanistan. No matter what the official Taliban line is, there will never be a true guarantee of safety for those individuals who worked with the American forces.

Furthermore, many Afghan refugees have only been given parolee status, which allows them to remain and work in the U.S. for a mere two years. If they have SIV cases, they will be able to adjust their status later and apply for permanent residency (Green Cards). Otherwise, they have to apply for asylum and prove that they would be killed if they returned to Afghanistan.

In addition to writing a personal statement, the parolees also need to present threat letters sent to them by the Taliban. This is essentially impossible. How can a person who is already in the U.S. expect to receive a threat letter from the Taliban?

This and many other issues will further complicate the process for all the parolees unless the U.S. government amends its policies. Even worse, those who have been separated from their families in the evacuation won't be able to bring their loved ones to America, as the requirement for doing so is either being a U.S. citizen or Green Card holder, neither of which the parolees can realize within the short time span allowed.

I am certainly one of the lucky ones. I made the right decision to leave on my own from the camp in Wisconsin and my family's documents were finally completed, except that we haven't yet received our green cards which could take up to half a year more. I first got my driver's license and then got my Commercial Driver's License (CDL/Class A) within six months of our arrival in California, and I plan on opening a truck company with my older brother and a few friends. However, the most important achievement so far has been the publishing of this book. It might have never gotten published had I not left Fort McCoy at the right time, or if I had not resettled in California.

Finding a place to rent was the greatest of all challenges. It wasn't (and still isn't) easy for many Afghan refugees to rent a house. And now with the refugees from Ukraine, the problem has gone from bad to worse. There aren't many houses for rent in the first place, and many landlords resist accepting applications from refugees who lack the required previous residence history in the U.S. Also, many can't prove they have income since they may not be able to find employment quickly after resettling. Therefore, the Afghan refugees must rely on their relatives and friends as cosigners or guarantors, but some housing communities don't even accept that arrangement.

Though there may still be opportunities to work with the U.S. military as a trilingual interpreter/translator, and I feel that I can really be of help with thousands of Afghans resettled across America, I won't be able to work in that capacity because employment with U.S. government agencies requires proof of citizenship and/or permanent residency, none of which I have. And jobs with non-government agencies would have prevented me (so far) from completing this book as well as obtaining my CDL, among other things.

Besides, I'll be helping my wife learn English, take the test for her driver's license (she just got her permit), and study in any field she wants to. She looks forward to working a job she enjoys where she can help others in the very best way. When I consider all the challenges we endured along our journey from Kabul to California, I give most of the credit for our success to Shazia. We wouldn't have made it through had she not been such a strong and caring wife and mother. My daughter still has a few years before she starts going to school, but we are sure she is a very smart girl and will thrive here in the U.S.

The fact that I have joined my brothers here in the U.S. also gives me a very contented feeling. I am so proud of them both. Afghan families are extremely tight-knit; there is no distinction between immediate and extended family members. My wife and I left our parents and siblings behind. We are unable to go back to spend time with them in Afghanistan, at least for the foreseeable future. For them, the immigration process will take years, so they can't come here either. We are praying every day that they will be safe.

CHAPTER NINE
THOUGHTS AND HOPES

November 21, 2021: With my family near the Golden Gate Bridge in San Francisco, California, USA.

Initially, when Russia's President Vladimir Putin ordered the invasion of Ukraine on February 24, 2022, most people, including political analysts and journalists in the West, made comparisons between that event and the Taliban's takeover of Afghanistan on August 15, 2021. Specifically, it was about how Afghan leaders fled the country and its military did not fight the Taliban while the Ukrainian leaders and armed forces have resisted so far. Of course, the current situation in Ukraine is especially painful for Afghans to witness. Ukraine is now experiencing what Afghanistan has been going through for over four decades—indiscriminate air bombardment, total destruction, influx of migrants

to other countries, prevalent poverty, and hunger threatening the lives of its citizenry. Like the rest of the world,
Afghans praise Ukraine's President Volodymyr Zelenskyy
and the Ukrainians for their bravery and resistance against
the Russian aggression.

When Ukraine agreed to completely denuclearize following its independence from the U.S.S.R., the U.S., the UK, and
the Soviet Union, entered into the 1994 agreement known
as the Budapest Memorandum, which guaranteed Ukraine's
security. Still, when Moscow annexed Ukraine's Crimea
Peninsula in 2014, Washington and London did nothing.
The U.S. and the EU continued to assure Ukraine that they
would stand firm with Kyiv if Moscow threatened, but even
after Putin deployed tens of thousands of troops to the
Ukraine border, Biden decided against sending American
troops to Ukraine. This emboldened Putin to turn what may
have been a military exercise—perhaps only meant to
threaten, not engage—into a full-scale invasion of Ukraine.

Many people in the West would be surprised to learn that
the citizens of Afghanistan and certainly its leaders, have a
deep general knowledge about the politics of the world, especially about the U.S., Europe, Russia, China, and its immediate neighbors Iran and Pakistan. But Americans and
Europeans know very little about what has been happening
in Afghanistan, despite the West's more than twenty years
of military and civilian engagement and presence in the
country. In my view, multiple similarities—and differences—exist regarding the plight of the Afghan people and
what the Ukrainians are now enduring.

First of all, from the start of the deployment of Soviet soldiers to Afghanistan in 1979 to the withdrawal of all U.S.
and other foreign troops from Afghanistan in mid-2021,

nearly three million Afghans died and another ten million were wounded. Upon the withdrawal by the Soviets, followed by the collapse of the Afghan government and a civil war between various mujahideen groups, the entire country was destroyed, and more than half of its residents were forced to flee its borders.

Upon the 2021 collapse of the Afghan government and the full withdrawal of American and other foreign troops, the exact same scenario played out again, except that a civil war did not take place this time mainly because the country was overtaken by a single group (the Taliban). In contrast, Ukraine and the Ukrainians haven't witnessed any of this. In other words, Afghans have been tired of years of constant wars, and therefore did not want to engage in another conflict of total bloodshed and destruction. But for the Ukrainians, it is the very first time, and they definitely wanted to resist with whatever means they had.

Secondly, Afghan government forces first fought for nearly ten years against the proxies of the U.S., Saudi Arabia, and Pakistan—the mujahideen—and then for nearly twenty years against the proxies of Russia, China, Iran, and Pakistan—the Taliban. However, if both the Soviet Union's aggression of 1979 and the U.S. attacks of 2001 are considered invasions (the Soviets *did* assassinate a sitting Afghan president and the U.S. *did* overthrow an Afghan government officially recognized by at least three countries), and the mujahideen and Taliban are considered pure Afghans (not proxies), then they have defeated two of the world's super powers—the Soviet Union and the U.S. (plus its allies), in the last forty years.

But in the case of Russia's invasion of Ukraine, it is one country against another—no proxies are involved. It is a direct military attack that has been condemned by a majority of countries worldwide. Now that we have seen this pervasive response and broad support for Ukraine, in hindsight we might say that perhaps its leaders and forces should have resisted Russia's initial aggression when it annexed Crimea in 2014. And while Afghanistan's existence has never been threatened in any form or condition, in the case of Ukraine, Putin blatantly seeks to revive the former Soviet Union, which would erase Ukraine's name (as an independent state) from the map and once again make it part of Russia. Given this blunt reality, Ukrainian leaders and armed forces *must* stand against Moscow's aggression and sacrifice everything to defend their independence, sovereignty, and territorial integrity.

Additionally, in a little more than four decades, three Afghan presidents were executed. Afghanistan's first president, Mohammad Daoud Khan, and his entire family (twenty-eight people) were assassinated in a coup in 1978. Hafizullah Amin (who had overthrown Dawood Khan) was killed by the Soviets the following year, and Mohammad Najibullah (who had sought refuge at the UN compound in Kabul for more than four years following his resignation and handing over of power to the U.S.-backed mujahideen), was publicly hanged to death by the Taliban in 1996. Hence, Ashraf Ghani would have probably been the next Afghan president killed by the enemy had he not fled the country. This hasn't ever happened in Ukraine. That has probably been the reason that Ukraine's President Volodymyr Zelenskyy has expressed no fear to stand steadfast alongside his forces and people to fight back against the Russians.

Moreover, the Taliban's fight against the U.S./West-backed government of Afghanistan over the past two decades employed indiscriminate suicide bombings and attacks on government offices, universities, schools, and hospitals. Any security policy would fail against such tactics. Besides, what can better describe bravery than wrestling down and overpowering suicide bombers? Members of the ANDSF did this hundreds of times when they identified an attacker, preventing the deaths of thousands. Furthermore, the ANDSF did not have a single fighter jet and were not allowed to use heavy weaponry against the Taliban in the first decade of the war (allegedly, to avoid civilian casualties). Also, in recent years, they were running short of supplies after the U.S. favored peace talks with the Taliban over fighting them militarily.

In the case of Ukraine, however, it is waging a conventional war against the Russians in the style of World War I and World War II. Kyiv has its own military that consists of tanks, fighter jets, and combat helicopters, and the Ukrainians are fighting the Russians in the air and on the ground. Ukraine's military and civilians have turned to guerrilla tactics as well, which has enabled them to successfully hamper the progress of Russia's ground troops. In this case, Ukraine's military and civilians are similar to the Afghan mujahideen who fought the Soviets, and the Taliban who waged a brutal war against Americans.

Moreover, Kyiv has been receiving a tremendous amount of support in other forms, such as financial and military aid and strong economic sanctions against Russia. But Afghanistan didn't enjoy anything close to this level of support, at least not in the last years of the war when America and its allies considered the Taliban a more reliable partner than the Afghan government. And in mid-2021, the whole world suddenly and abruptly abandoned the Afghans.

Similarly, the world also remained silent when the U.S. and the UK invaded Iraq in 2003, allegedly to neutralize Saddam Hussain and capture his suspected Weapons of Mass Destruction (WMD), but of course it turned out that there never were any WMDs in Iraq. In addition, Israel's years-long occupation of Palestinian territories has been rarely criticized by world powers. But when Ukraine, a non-Muslim and non-Arab country was invaded by Russia, we saw an entirely different response. In this case, almost the entire world has stood behind Kyiv and against Moscow.

Not only that, following the Arab Spring in Tunisia, Libya, Syria, Egypt, and Yemen, and in response to the continuing wars in Iraq and Afghanistan, hundreds of thousands of Muslim refugees fled to Europe in the last decade. Many drowned in oceans while more were killed attempting to cross borders of various countries, many of which refused to take them in. Worse than that, during the chaotic evacuation from Kabul in mid-2021, approximately 130,000 Afghans were taken to numerous countries around the world, and thousands still remain in various refugee camps in the UAE, Qatar, Pakistan, EU countries and elsewhere. Among them are SIV applicants, members of Afghanistan's Zero units, and Afghan citizens. Contrary to this, Europeans quickly opened their arms to warmly welcome the Ukrainians, and the U.S. swiftly made changes to its refugee/immigration policies to avoid deportation of Ukrainians already in America and to bring in those at risk in Ukraine. The UK government even offered to give 350 pounds per month to any family willing to house Ukrainian refugees.

The main similarity between the Ukraine war and the Afghanistan situation is that the flow of hundreds of foreign fighters into Ukraine is identical to the flow of thousands of

Islamist fighters that went to Afghanistan in the late 1980s and beyond. They first fought alongside the Afghan mujahideen who were fighting the Soviets. When the Taliban movement began fighting the mujahideen, more and more Arab fighters joined them. Even after twenty years of the U.S. and NATO military presence in Afghanistan, official reports of Afghanistan's Ministry of Defense pointed to more than twenty foreign terrorist groups operating in the country, including Al-Qaeda, ISIS-K (ISIS-Khurasan, the terrorist group's branch operating in the border areas between Afghanistan and Pakistan), the Islamic Movement of Uzbekistan (IMU), and Lashkar-e-Jhangvi (a Sunni extremist group founded in Pakistan).

On the other hand, the problems facing Afghan evacuees around the world has multiplied in the months since the evacuation of Kabul was completed. The U.S. government failed to manage their retreat from Afghanistan properly, both at the point of evacuation and in its aftermath. The general view among most Afghans is that the U.S. government wasn't prepared and the U.S. military wasn't trained to manage a humanitarian crisis on such a large scale. Most feel the evacuation of Afghanistan was flawed from the beginning and hasn't shown any signs of improvement since.

With respect to how American leaders are viewed in Afghanistan, in general, Afghan people and leaders have preferred republican presidents over democrats in the White House. We felt that they supported America's military engagement in Afghanistan, which enabled our country to rise above Taliban rule. President Bush was famous among Afghans for overthrowing the Taliban regime and President Trump was hailed for announcing a *condition-based* withdrawal of U.S. troops from Afghanistan at a critical time of the war. Though President Obama was loved among the educated Afghans for his long, well-structured, and inspiring speeches around the world, Afghan leaders did not like his stance on Afghanistan.

President Biden has never been a favorite among Afghans. Even when he was the vice-president in Obama's administration, we felt he preferred Pakistan over Afghanistan. After becoming president, Biden was strongly criticized for saying, "Never has Afghanistan been a united country, not at all in its history," and "No nation has ever unified Afghanistan." His announcement of the full withdrawal of American troops from Afghanistan made him a target of critics in Afghanistan and around the world. Worst of all, Biden's decision of February 12, 2022, to give half of Afghanistan's $7 billion reserves to the victims of the 9/11 attacks infuriated many Afghans.

The democrat presidents were not our favorites for another important reason—their stance regarding Pakistan. Even after Osama Bin Laden was killed by U.S. Navy SEALs in the heart of Pakistan, President Obama did not take action against Pakistan for providing him sanctuary. Conversely, Trump put a hold on U.S. military aid to Pakistan in order to force it to take strong actions against terrorists that targeted the ANDSF and American troops in Afghanistan.

Coming back to the collapse of the Afghan government, though the Taliban took control of the entire country in only eleven days, the fall of President Ashraf Ghani's government was gradual. It actually began years before when the U.S. started making concessions to the Taliban like downgrading the organization from "terrorist group" to "insurgent group," and allowing negotiations to occur between the two (because the U.S. officially maintains a policy of refusal to negotiate with terrorists). They also granted the Taliban permission to open a political office in Doha (Qatar) and remove the names of senior Taliban leaders from the UN and America's blacklists. They released Mullah Abdul Ghani Baradar, the Taliban's chief negotiator and current vice-chairman of the Taliban government from a Pakistani prison, seriously marginalized Ashraf Ghani and his government from the ensuing peace talks, pressured President Ghani to free five thousand Taliban militants from Afghan prisons, and cut military and logistical support to the ANDSF in early 2021.

Even worse, the U.S. fulfilled all its commitments to the Taliban before the latter made any concessions either to the U.S. or the Afghan government. And when the time approached for the Taliban to deliver on their promises, Biden announced the full withdrawal of his troops from Afghanistan. This, on one hand, significantly weakened Afghanistan's stance against the Taliban, both on the battlefield and at the negotiating table, and on the other hand, emboldened the terrorist group to quickly gain more ranks by declaring amnesty to anyone who surrendered to the group. In fact, the ANDSF were never defeated militarily, but the government collapsed as a result of this political conspiracy.

Truthfully, though Biden's decision to withdraw all U.S. forces may be the main reason for the collapse of Afghanistan and the return of the Taliban to power, it *was not* the only one. Afghan leaders are equally to be blamed. To start with, the President, Ashraf Ghani, may have been a lecturer, minister, politician, and president, but he certainly wasn't a leader, and his mistakes were legion.

When he nominated himself for the elections, his name was Mohammad Ashraf Ghani Ahmadzai. There are two

Ahmadzai tribes in southeastern Afghanistan: Afghanistan's former President Najibullah belonged to the one in Paktia province, and Ashraf Ghani was born in the neighboring Logar Province. While serving as Afghanistan's Minister of Finance, Chancellor of Kabul University, and Chairman of Transition Commission (transfer of responsibility of security from foreign troops to the ANDSF), Ghani had become a well-known figure among all Afghans, but most people voted for him because of his last name, Ahmadzai, believing he would serve the country as faithfully as Najibullah had done. However, on his second day in office, he officially removed "Ahmadzai" from his last name. As a result, many people realized that he had deceived them, and that he had only used the last name to get as many votes as possible.

In addition, Ashraf Ghani had surrounded himself with young people who did not have any previous experience in governance, much less in the military and intelligence fields. For example, his national security advisor, Hamdullah Mohib, had a degree in computer system engineering from Brunel University in London. But in order to develop effective wartime policies in a country like Afghanistan, where multiple domestic and foreign proxy groups had waged a relentless battle against both Afghan forces and the people, the second person (after the president) needed to have an indepth knowledge of what was happening.

Mohib had *never* served in the military or intelligence branches of the government before becoming Ashraf Ghani's national security advisor. And in the civilian sector of the government, the president was served by Fazal Mahmood Fazli, head of the administrative office of the president. Fazli had his say in almost all affairs pertaining to the civilian agencies of the Afghan government. Overall, Ashraf Ghani only listened to these two figures and saw Afghanistan's situation through their eyes, but the problem was that these two were very corrupt and did not share the facts with the president. Now, it seems that Mohib and Fazli might have forced President Ghani to flee the country because otherwise, they wouldn't have been able to flee on their own.

Amrullah Saleh, the first vice-president under Ashraf Ghani, had years of experience in the war and intelligence from the years of serving (allegedly as an interpreter) with Ahmad Shah Massoud, the leader of Afghanistan's Northern Alliance during the jihad against the Soviets and the civil war. He also had dealt with various intelligence agencies during Afghanistan's civil war, led Afghanistan's National Directorate of Security (NDS), the equivalent of the CIA and the FBI combined for over six years, and searched for Osama Bin Laden in Pakistan's tribal regions. The worst thing about Saleh's role as the vice-president was that he focused on activities that should have been dealt with by Kabul's municipality, like how to get the city cleaned, what needed to be done to remove the vendors from the streets, how to gather addicts from across the city, and more. He should have led the fight against the Taliban, especially since becoming the vice-president.

With regard to engaging with the U.S. and the Taliban, Ashraf Ghani never told the nation what America and the Taliban really wanted from the years-long peace talks. He only thought about his own grip on power. Had he told Afghans that the U.S. was making secret deals with the Taliban, the entire country would have stood behind him and would have fought the Taliban, even with their bare hands.

President Ghani was nice to everybody and loved large gatherings of people where he talked for hours. His easy stance against former warlords and members of parliament who had turned into the biggest challengers to the government allowed them to become the biggest criminals across the country. Worst of all, on the evening of August 12, 2021 (three days before his government collapsed) Herat, an economic hub in the west of Afghanistan with over two million people and an ANA Corps of more than fifteen thousand soldiers fell to the Taliban, but at that very same evening, President Ghani was lecturing thousands of youths at the Presidential Palace who had gathered to celebrate International Youth Day. It was *the* time he should have spent focusing on, at the very least, how to prevent the capital from being overrun by the Taliban, and absolutely *not* the right time to celebrate Youth Day.

Moreover, the ANDSF and the public believed that when the time came, all high-ranking government officials, leaders of the opposition parties, politicians, and former warlords would stand together against the Taliban because that is what they had been saying for years. Instead, they fled the country within hours, even faster than they had in the mid-1990s when the Taliban first appeared.

I voted for Ashraf Ghani in both presidential elections and attended a number of gatherings where he spoke. I even have a picture with him. What made him different from other Afghan leaders was his academic background (a professor of anthropology at Johns Hopkins University), international profile (years of experience at World Bank) and the fact that he was never involved in any form in Afghanistan's civil war. Also, he had done pretty well in his previous assignments. However, what he did at the end led to a legacy that he and no one else wanted to be marked in the history of Afghanistan. *He shouldn't have fled the country.*

In an interview he gave to the BBC months after the fall of Kabul to the Taliban, Ashraf Ghani said that he wanted to go to Khost, a southeastern province of Afghanistan. In eastern and southern Afghanistan where most of the population are Pashton, it is a common tribal and traditional principal that if a person seeks shelter at one's house, he will not be handed over to his enemies at any cost—a code of Pashtonwali (being Pashton).

For example, in 2005, a four-man team of U.S. Navy SEALs was deployed on a reconnaissance mission to Afghanistan's eastern Kunar Province. While hidden in the bushes, they were spotted by a few locals who had taken their herd of animals out to the mountains. The SEALs decided not to capture or kill them, but the locals later informed the Taliban. Sometime later, hundreds of militants stormed the mountainous area to kill or capture the SEALs alive.

Three of the SEALs were killed in the first hours of the battle, but Marcus Luttrell dramatically survived. In 2007, he wrote a book, *Lone Survivor*, about his accounts of the incident, and in 2013, a Hollywood movie based on the book was released starring Mark Wahlberg as Marcus Luttrell.

In the movie, while drinking water from a stream, Luttrell encounters a local Afghan and his son. They offer him shelter, food and clothes, treat his wounds, and alert a U.S. Army base in the area. The Taliban still keep looking for him and before the Americans arrive to rescue him, a fierce fight takes place between the Taliban and the locals who refuse to hand Luttrell over to them, claiming that he sought refuge with them. More than ten locals were killed by the Taliban before an American gunship and multiple helicopters arrived to eliminate the threat and evacuate Luttrell.

There is a similar story about the Taliban and the group's founder, Mullah Mohammad Omar. It's said that when the U.S. asked the Taliban to hand over Al-Qaeda leader Osama Bin Laden to America, the Taliban denied doing so only to honor the principal of Pashtonwali. They were prepared to lose the government (and country) just to adhere to the tribal rule of protecting a refuge seeker. This account of the story was narrated on April 24, 2022, by the Taliban's current spokesperson at the ceremony to commemorate the ninth year of the death of their supreme leader, Mullah Mohammad Omar.

Likewise, Ashraf Ghani might have thought that by seeking refuge in Khost Province, locals would protect him from any harm by the Taliban. Though there was no guarantee that the Taliban would not publicly execute him because they never fulfilled the promises they made, him fleeing the country wasn't worth what the Afghans and Afghanistan have been dealing with over the past year, with probably many more years to come. Some of this might have been prevented had he stayed in the country.

Also, it is worth noting that the Taliban are now stronger than before in many ways. Prior to 2001, there were around half the number of Taliban militants in Afghanistan than there are now. They controlled less territory than they do now, and they had fewer weapons than they have now (much less American military assets worth $7 billion, including aircraft).

They were recognized by only three countries in the world compared to the formal and informal support they now have among regional powers who are archrivals of the U.S.—Russia, China, and Iran (let alone Pakistan, the biggest and most vocal supporter of the Taliban).

On the other hand, the world cannot and shall not remain indifferent. Now, it's *not* only about the Taliban. The lives of thirty million Afghans are at stake. The past two decades have revealed that a military solution does not work for Afghanistan. Therefore, the world *must* engage with the Taliban, and both shall agree on certain issues. In this case, the international community, and above all the U.S., must obtain strong and written guarantees from the Taliban that they will respect, observe, and protect all norms of human rights laws before any financial support to Afghanistan is offered. Moreover, the Taliban must prove to the Afghan people that they are not Pakistan's puppets, and must also promise, in writing, that they will grant access to investigations of any human rights abuses/violations alleged by the UN. It is worth noting that any financial aid must be distributed through international organizations directly to Afghans, not the Taliban government.

With regard to the influence of the U.S. in the world, the complete, abrupt, and chaotic withdrawal of American forces from Afghanistan and the relative inaction regarding Moscow's invasion of Ukraine have significantly damaged America's image on the global stage, and has weakened its status as a superpower, leading Japan, South Korea, Taiwan, and other U.S. allies to consider new strategic agreements with other major world powers. On June 29, 2022, a Chinese government official put two pictures on his twitter account; one showing an American C-17 military plane running over people on the tarmac at Kabul airport following the fall of Kabul in August 2021, and a Chinese military plane loaded with humanitarian assistance packages for the victims of a recent earthquake in southeastern Afghanistan. His caption read, "Two military planes showed up at Kabul airport, one taking life and the other carrying hope. This is perhaps the biggest difference between China and the U.S."

On a personal note, like thousands of other Afghan evacuees, I am just happy to be alive, and grateful that my family and I made it successfully through the ordeal. I know that the experiences of working with U.S. and NATO forces in Afghanistan for eight years were crucial in meeting the challenges of our long and frustrating journey which required not just mental and physical strength, but insight and understanding of both Western culture and military processes. We are now adjusting to our new home in America and look to the future with hope, reverence, and love.

But it is a sad fact that I won't be able to return to Afghanistan any time in the foreseeable future. The conditions on the ground there are dangerous in general, and particularly hazardous for me personally as an interpreter who worked with perceived "infidels", and especially because of my employment with American and other foreign forces in Afghanistan, and now, because of this book, in which I not only criticize both U.S. President Joe Biden and former Afghan President Ashraf Ghani, but also aim my finger at the Taliban.

Last but not least, Kashmir, a lush region between India and Pakistan, is famous for its beautiful natural landscapes, and the name has long graced the literature and poetry of Afghanistan. One such proverb in Pashto language declares, *"Har-Cha Ta Khpal Watan Kashmir Dai,"* which translates as, "For everybody, his/her homeland is Kashmir." It's the same story for me when it comes to Afghanistan.

For decades, Afghan civilians have suffered from a civil war, indiscriminate air strikes, suicide attacks, roadside and remote-controlled IEDs, insurgent attacks in public places, and many more horrors. Businessmen or their children were kidnapped for ransom. Robberies were normal, day and night, and people were killed if they resisted the thieves. Warlords were so powerful, that they, their sons, and their armed bodyguards bullied ordinary people on the streets of Kabul on a daily basis. They weren't held responsible even if they killed a policeman in broad daylight. The stealing of vehicle number plates was rampant, and that left such a lingering psychological effect that still, even though I am now in the U.S., I check constantly to make sure my car's plates are there. But at the end of the day, Afghanistan is Kashmir for me and every other Afghan. Consequently, no matter how far or how long I am away, I will always have Afghanistan in my heart, and to my homeland and people, I offer my prayers.

Chapter Ten
Postscript

An Afghan school girl crying during a live TV interview after Taliban, without a prior notice, banned girls beyond 6th grade to attend schools. Tolo News photo.

After one year of the chaotic withdrawal of all foreign troops from Afghanistan and as my story gets published, thousands of Afghans are still left with unpredictable futures in camps in various countries and hundreds of SIV applicants are still languishing in Afghanistan. I hope this book persuades Americans to put more pressure on the Biden administration to make quick changes to the U.S. refugee and immigration policies and thereby help Afghan refugees relocate to the U.S. as soon as possible.

And what no one seems to be noticing is that with the war in Ukraine, Afghanistan has once again been forgotten by the world while a humanitarian crisis is unfolding there.

In a blatant disregard for the promises made during peace talks with the U.S. and unfruitful phases of negotiations with representatives of the former government of Afghanistan, the Taliban have been rolling back most of the significant achievements made by Afghans in the past twenty years. Below are examples:

Targeted Killings of Afghan Government Forces

On November 30, 2021, the *Washington Post* reported that the Taliban were waging a campaign of targeted killings against former members of the ANDSF. The article claimed that, "The killings come despite a pledge to grant amnesty to former Afghan security forces and government officials, demonstrating that building international pressure for the group to respect human rights has done little to sway the Taliban from the use of indiscriminate violence to respond to groups and individuals perceived as threats."

The Taliban, right after taking control of Kabul in August 2021, declared a national amnesty to anyone who had served in the ranks of the ANDSF or in the civilian sectors of the West-backed government of Afghanistan. However, as days passed, horrifying videos of Taliban militants killing former members of the ANDSF began circulating on social media. Since the Taliban's takeover, hundreds of such incidents have been documented by human rights agencies and reported by local and international media. Most former members of the ANDSF have either left the country or changed their names, locations, and mobile phones so they cannot be tracked by the Taliban. But it hasn't been difficult for the Taliban to find them as the records of all government employees are now in their hands because former Afghan government staff didn't have time to destroy them. And even if Taliban leadership remains committed to the amnesty, they are helpless to prevent their low-ranking militants from committing crimes against former members of the ANDSF.

Suppression of Women's Rights and Freedoms

On January 24, 2022, the *New York Times* reported that the Taliban were threatening and beating women who were protesting their harsh rule, saying, "The Taliban have begun cracking down harder as women insist on their rights and as Western governments call for reforms," and that "Taliban gunmen have pointed weapons at the demonstrators, sprayed them with pepper spray and called them 'whores' and 'puppets of the West.'"

On March 23, 2022, *The Guardian* reported that the Taliban "are facing international condemnation after they announced on Wednesday that girls would not be allowed to attend secondary and high school, despite their previous assurances." They quoted UN High Commissioner for Human Rights, Michelle Bachelet, who said the decision was "of grave concern at a time when the country desperately needs to overcome multiple intersecting crises. Disempowering half of Afghanistan's population is counterproductive and unjust." It has already been over a full education year (310 days) that girls haven't been able to attend classes over 6th grade.

On March 28, 2022, the *Associated Press* and the *Star Tribune* reported that "Taliban hard-liners are turning back the clock" in Afghanistan with a spate of authoritarian edicts that recall their harsh rule in the 1990s. They stated that

Afghan girls have been banned from going to school beyond the sixth grade, women were being barred from boarding planes when travelling unaccompanied by a male relative, men and women could only visit public parks on separate days, and that the use of mobile telephones in universities has been prohibited.

On May 7, 2022, the *New York Times* described how the Taliban were imposing head-to-toe coverings for women. The article claimed that the decree by the Ministry for the Propagation of Virtue and the Prevention of Vice, "drew condemnation from women's rights advocates and the United Nations, which described it as another bald betrayal of Taliban pledges to respect gender equality."

On May 22, 2022, *Aljazeera* reported that Taliban ordered all female anchors on Afghan TV channels to cover their faces. Taliban's Ministry of Information and Culture said that the order was "final and non-negotiable".

After taking control of Afghanistan, the Taliban quickly banned women from going to offices. Only female doctors and nurses were allowed to go to work. Later, as the Taliban began providing services to the people, they realized that they needed to allow more women to work. Therefore, they eased the rules a little bit. But it hasn't been to the scale it used to be during the former government. For instance, now, women cannot serve in the ranks of security forces or in high-ranking and senior government positions. When human and women's rights activists protested the discrimination in the streets of Kabul, the Taliban suppressed them immediately and brutally.

Worst of all so far has been the ban on girls' education. The Taliban, without any prior notice, refused to allow girls beyond the sixth grade (secondary classes) to attend school.

To justify their action, the Taliban claimed that the uniforms of the schoolgirls did not conform to traditional Islamic and Afghan values. The restrictions did not stop there. The Taliban later decreed that no woman could travel a distance further than forty-five miles (seventy-two kilometers) without a male companion, and that drivers of taxis and buses should not offer rides to women without a proper hijab. Furthermore, the group ordered all domestic airlines and airport staff to not allow women that weren't accompanied by male guardians onto planes.

In addition, the Taliban's Ministry for the Propagation of Virtue and the Prevention of Vice specified separate days for men and women to visit parks, which of course meant that families wouldn't be able to enjoy parks together. Following that, the Taliban issued another decree stating, "If a woman does not follow the rules, her male guardian will be visited and advised, and eventually jailed and sentenced. Also, women who work in government offices and do not follow the new decree will be fired." And in their most recent move, the Taliban warned all TV channels to fire their female presenters if they do not cover their faces while on TV.

The crackdown has not stopped with women. On March 28, 2022, *The Hill* reported that the Taliban were requiring beards and a strict dress code for male government workers in addition to multiple other restrictions that, "echo scenes from their previous rule in the 1990s." They claimed that "Employees are instructed not to shave their beards and are required to wear clothing consisting of long, loose tops and trousers, as well as a hat or turban," and that "the workers risk being fired if they do not adhere to the requirement."

Crackdown on Freedom of Speech

In January 2022, the *Wall Street Journal* reported the Taliban were intensifying their "crackdown on dissent" and had begun arresting and executing prominent Afghans for criticizing the regime, including Faizullah Jalal, Kabul University professor who had gained national fame for berating a senior Taliban official on live television.

In April 2022, *Reporters Without Borders* said that journalists were being increasingly harassed by Taliban intelligence. They claimed that "the Taliban intelligence agency known as the 'Istikhbarat' and the Ministry for the Propagation of Virtue and the Prevention of Vice are directly implicated in this harassment, which violates Afghanistan's press law."

On March 18, 2022, CBS reported that Taliban intelligence had arrested three staff members of TOLO TV, one of Afghanistan's largest private television stations, because they objected to a story they broadcast. They stated that the arrests were met with "international outcry, including broader demands from the UN and the Committee to Protect Journalists (CPJ) for the country's rulers to stop harassing local journalists and stifling free expression through threats, arrests, and intimidation."

On March 28, 2022, the *Business Standard* reported on the Taliban's decision to ban international media from airing in Afghanistan and claimed that since the Taliban regained control of the country in August 2021, 40 percent of Afghan media outlets—an estimated 6,400 journalists—had become unemployed, while "more than eighty percent of Afghan female journalists have also lost their jobs since the fall of Kabul."

The Taliban regime claims its legitimacy derives from Islam and Sharia (the Islamic legal system). Accordingly, most Taliban militants don't receive any salary for their services. They are told that they are soldiers of Allah and that they are serving for a greater cause than worldly wealth. As a result, most Taliban militants consider their leaders to be saints, sinless, and free from guilt. Therefore, anyone who criticizes the Taliban government is considered an enemy of Islam, an "infidel" committing a grave sin, and they face harsh reprisals—detainment, prison, and even execution.

The Taliban banned UK's BBC, America's *Voice of America* (VOA), China's *Global Television Network* (CGTN), and Germany's *Deutsche Welle* (DW), the four international networks that aired via multiple private television channels in Afghanistan broadcasting in Pashto, Dari, and Uzbeki. The Taliban have ordered the Afghan affiliates to stop airing news bulletins from these four major world media outlets.

The Forgotten Afghan Refugees

On February 15, 2022, the *Jerusalem Post* reported on forgotten Afghan refugees who were languishing in refugee camps not knowing when they would be allowed to leave. They stated that Afghan refugees being held in camps in Dubai in the UAE had been protesting every day for the last week over their frozen status as they waited to receive a visa and be transferred to the U.S., which they say they were promised when America withdrew from Afghanistan in August 2021.

On April 5, 2022, NPR reported on Afghan families that were split up during the evacuation and were still waiting to be reunited with their loved ones. They claimed that "The U.S. and its NATO partners promised to get Afghans whom they'd trained, armed, and funded out of Kabul last summer along with their families. This included Afghan soldiers, interpreters, and advisers directly employed by the U.S.—and those who worked for U.S. and NATO-funded organizations and projects. Because of their affiliation with Western powers, these Afghans are in danger of persecution by the Taliban."

On April 9, 2022, NBC reported that Afghans attempting to enter the U.S. to escape Taliban rule are subject to stricter requirements than Ukrainians seeking refuge from the Russian invasion. They said that thousands of Afghans—even some threatened by the Taliban—have been rejected, and quoted Matt Zeller, a senior advisor to Iraq and Afghanistan Veterans of America (IAVA), saying, "There are clearly two refugee systems, one for Ukrainians and one for Afghans. Afghans are our longest wartime ally ever. You'd think we'd want to do right by them."

As the Taliban made their way into Kabul on August 15, 2021, the U.S. and its allies began the Vietnam-style evacuation of their Afghan partners. The evacuees were first taken to various camps across the world from where they were supposed to resettle in America, Canada and Europe. One of the largest refugee camps for Afghans was in the UAE. However, as the initial phase of the evacuation was completed, the U.S. government, facing various policy and administrative challenges, decided to essentially halt the resettlement process.

As of the date of the completion of this book, thousands of Afghan refugees still remain at refugee camps in the UAE, Qatar, Pakistan and some EU countries. Many decided to return home despite fears of Taliban reprisals. Most of those evacuated in August 2021 were men who left behind entire families. Many of them were the primary breadwinners for their families who quickly ran out of money. For them, the only choice was to return to Afghanistan so they could once again support their families. Worse than that, those leaving the camp in the UAE have been asked to sign documents saying they won't be at risk back in Afghanistan. If they refuse, they aren't allowed to leave the camp.

On July 14, 2022, "CBC News" reported that Canada has decided to close the special Afghan immigration program to new applicants. According to the report, "Ottawa has only processed 15,000 applications and will continue processing 3,000 others who already applied for the program. Less than halfway to its goal of bringing 40,000 Afghans to Canada, the federal government is no longer taking new referrals for the special program meant to prioritize former employees of the Canadian Armed Forces or government and their families". CBC News quoted Lauryn Oates, the executive director of Canadian Women 4 Women in Afghanistan, as saying, "They (Afghans) have tried everything else. They have knocked on the doors of other governments, other embassies, all kinds of other programs. They are trapped and they are in danger".

Fear of Civil War and International Terrorism

On April 11, 2022 *Foreign Policy* reported that an armed resistance has begun against the Taliban. According to the report, many former political figures and military leaders of the former Afghan government have recruited fighters from the ranks of the former armed forces of Afghanistan, mostly trained by the US and its allies. Though Taliban fighters have continuously been targeted in different parts of the country, the main armed opposition is launched by the National Resistance Front (NRF) led by Ahmad Massoud, the son of former Mujahideen commander Ahmad Shah Massoud. Former First Vice-President, Amrullah Saleh, has also been guiding NRF fighters against the Taliban. The Taliban on their part, however, has repeatedly denied the existence of any armed resistance though some local news agencies in Afghanistan have been quoting sources that Taliban have launched massive military operations in Panjshir, the main stronghold of NRF, and have committed serous human rights violations there. In his most recent interview with the BBC on July 11, 2022, Ahmad Massoud said that his forces number at nearly 3,000.

Besides, there have been reports of conflicts between different groups of the Taliban as well. Mawlawi Mahdi Mujahid, commander of a group of Taliban that mainly belong to the Hazara ethnic group, has began fighting the regime, allegedly for trying to sideline him.

On June 30, 2022, The Taliban convened a three-day traditional Loya Jirga (Grand Assembly) in Kabul. According to the Taliban controlled Radio and Television of Afghanistan (RTA), more than 3,000 religious clerks and tribal elders attended the assembly, the purpose of which according to the Taliban, was to get advice from the Afghan nation on how things should be run. Surprisingly, no women, former government officials, representatives of the youth and opposition groups were invited to the gathering which took place behind closed doors. There was no live broadcast of the Jirga either, but short voice clips of the statements made by various speakers were shared on RTA's

Facebook page. In one of the clips, Mujib Rahman Ansari, an Imam from Western Herat province, said, "anyone who stands against this government (the Taliban) shall be beheaded".

On May 27, 2022, *Business Standard* reported that the United Nations Security Council (UNSC) has found out that Al-Qaeda, the terrorist network behind the 9/11 attacks in the U.S., has once again pledged allegiance to the Taliban. According to the UNSC report, "180 to 400 fighters affiliated with Al-Qaeda from Bangladesh, India, Myanmar and Pakistan are settled in Afghanistan".

The Neglected Nation

The plight of Afghanistan and its unfolding humanitarian crisis was quickly replaced by other stories, and in this case, the Ukraine-Russia conflict, in major media in the West. Though some news outlets are referencing the current struggles of the Afghan people, they are few and far between. It is as if the West wants to forget the entire affair; the U.S. government certainly wants to forget the botched evacuation. But though the crisis in Ukraine is unquestionably dire and its people deserve unswerving support from the global community, the same consideration must apply to the Afghan people. There is an unquestionable and very concerning double standard regarding the response to these two global challenges. While the U.S. should offer any and all support to the Ukrainians, they cannot ignore the repression and poverty now facing Afghans, a quandary that the U.S., in many ways, created.

It is long past time for the U.S. and its Western allies to stand tall for Afghanistan, a country thirsting for freedom

145

and democracy, whose people have worked alongside Western forces for twenty years to affect positive change and future relationships with the nations of the world. The people of the world mustn't let the Afghan people—with their hardships, challenges, and vast potential—recede from our memories, or be neglected in our attention and efforts.

For updated information,
news, and resources,
visit
PromisesBetrayed.com

PHOTO GALLERY

SERVING WITH COALITION FORCES

2008 – On my first mission with Italian forces in Ghuryan district, Herat, Afghanistan. I always tried to keep everybody entertained, whether on the base or on the mission.

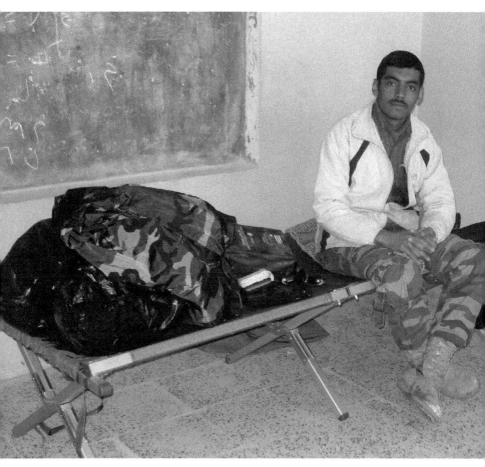

2008 – During the mission at Ghuryan district, Herat, Afghanistan. The Coalition Forces did not have a base in the area. Therefore, the school in the district bazaar was used to accommodate ANDSF and Coalition Forces during the mission.

2008 – On my second mission with Italian forces in Shindand district, Herat, Afghanistan. The ANA's 207th Corps Commander Major General (MG/Two-Star) Jalandar Shah Behnam (center) visited the Soviet-era airfield in the district for an initial inspection in order to prepare it for future use by ANDSF and Coalition Forces. It later became one of the largest training fields for Afghan Air Force (AAF).

2008 – On a mission with Italian forces along the highway from Herat to Qala-e-Naw, the provincial capital of Badghis province, Afghanistan.

2008 – On a city tour with ANA's 207th Corps Commander MG Fazl Ahmad Sayar (left) and his Italian advisor Colonel (Col.) Giovannini at the historical citadel in Herat, Afghanistan.

2009 – Providing linguistic services for then-Lieutenant General (LG/Three-Star) Giuseppe Valotto of the Italian Ministry of Defense at the Change of Command ceremony of ISAF's Regional Command (RC)-West, Herat, Afghanistan.

2008 – At the Change-of-Command ceremony of Afghan Regional Security Integration Command (ARSIC) – West, Herat, Afghanistan.
From left to right:
MG Ikramuddin Yawar, Commander of Afghan National Police (ANP); Shoaib, Afghan-American interpreter of the ARSIC-West Commander; Italian Army Col. Giam Zuca Giovannini, advisor to the ANA's 207th Corps Commander; MG Jalandar Shah Behnam, Commander of ANA's 207th Corps; US Army Col. Jim Klingaman, the outgoing ARSIC-West Commander; Italian Air Force Brigadier General (BG/One-Star) Arena, Commander of RC-West; and me.

2008 – With the escorts of Italian Army Col. Giovannini, whom I worked with as an interpreter, in Herat, Afghanistan.

2009 – With MG Fazl Ahmad Sayar, ANA's 207th Corps Commander, at Qala-e-Naw Airfield, Badghis province, Afghanistan. Two weeks later, MG Sayar died when his helicopter crashed due to bad weather.

*2009 – With Italian Army Col. Ignazio
Gamba, advisor to ANA's 207th Corps
Commander, Herat, Afghanistan.*

2009 – US Army General (Four-Star) David Petraeus (left), then-Commander of Central Command (CENTCOM), MG Jalandar Shah Behnam, ANA's 207th Corps Commander (center) and US Army Col. John Bessler (right), ARSIC-West Commander – during the visit of General Petraeus of the ANA Corps, Herat, Afghanistan.

2009 – During the visit of General David Petraeus at the office of ANA's 207th Corps Commander. The purpose of the visit was to assess security situation in the region and discuss aspects of counter-insurgency (COIN) on which General Petraeus had written a guidance for Coalition Forces in Afghanistan.

*2009 – With General David Petraeus
during his visit at ANA's 207th Corps,
Herat, Afghanistan.*

2009 – At the office of ANA's 207th Corps Commander with Italian Army Col. Ignazio Gamba (right) and four members of ANA (left) who were set free by the Taliban. The Afghan soldiers were captured in a Taliban ambush in Badghis province, Afghanistan, and were released after months-long negotiations brokered by local elders and tribal leaders. Taliban used to make prisoners of war (POWs) grow beard and give them traditional Afghan clothes at the time of their release.

2009 – Providing linguistic services at a security meeting in the yard of the office of the provincial governor of Farah province, Afghanistan. Senior officials including; MG Jalandar Shah Behnam, Commander of ANA's 207th Corps; Rohullah Amin, governor of Farah; US Marine Commander; US Provincial Reconstruction Team (PRT) Commander and representatives of the intelligence community were among the participants of the meeting.

2009 – *During a mission in Bakwa area of Farah province, Afghanistan.*

*2009 – With US Army Col. John Bessler,
Commander of ARSIC-West in Herat, Afghanistan.*

2009 – Interpreting for ANA's 207th Corps Commander MG Jalandar Shah Behnam (right) and his advisor Italian Army Col. Ignazio Gamba (left) during a Civil-Military Cooperation (CIMIC) mission in Herat, Afghanistan.

2009 – Chatting with Italian Army Col. Ignazio Gamba (center) while having lunch in a traditional Afghan way (setting down with legs folded) during a CIMIC mission in Herat, Afghanistan. The villagers served us Shurbaa (also pronounced Shurwaa), a typical Afghan dish.

2009 – Providing linguistic support to then-MG of the US Army, Richard P. Formica (left), Commander of Combined Security Transition Command – Afghanistan (CSTC-A), and ANA Brigadier General (One-Star) Zeyarat Shah Abed (right), Commander of 1st Brigade of 207th Corps during a visit of MG Formica to Herat, Afghanistan.

2009 – At Qala-e-Naw Airfield, Badghis province,
Afghanistan. In the background are two Italian
Air Force helicopters known as Agusta.

*2009 – Onboard a Russian Mi-17 helicopter
of the AAF. Next to me is ANA's 207th Corps
Command Sergeant Major (CSM).*

2009 – On a mission with MG Jalandar Shah Behnam, ANA's 207th Corps Commander (center) and his Italian advisor Col. Ignazio Gamba (second right) in Bakwa area of Southwestern Farah province, Afghanistan. The mission was focused on assessing the condition of ANA's Forward Operating Bases (FOBs) along Afghanistan's ring road, also known as Highway One (HW1).

2009 – During a mission on a Coalition Forces base in Farah province, Afghanistan. This was one of the first Humvees (also known as HMMWV/High Mobility Multipurpose Wheeled Vehicles) given to the ANA. The weapon on the Humvee is called DShk (Dishka) – a Russian equivalent of American M2 Browning 50 Caliber machine gun.

2009 – Providing linguistic services for MG Jalanadar Shah Behnam (left), ANA's 207th Corps Commander, and BG Paolo Serra (right), RC-West Commander, Herat, Afghanistan.

2009 – Interpreting for Italian Army BG Paolo Serra (right), RC-West Commander and Italian Army Col. Ignazio Gamba (left), advisor to ANA's 207th Corps Commander, Herat, Afghanistan.

2009 – With MG Jalandar Shah Behnam (left), Commander of ANA's 207th Corps, US Army Col. John Bessler (center), Commander of ARSIC-West, and Italian Army Col. Ignazio Gamba (right), advisor to the 207th Corps Commander at Herat's ancient Great Blue Mosque. Afghan counterparts of Coalition Forces would take the latter on a tour of the historical sites of Herat city at the end of their mission in Afghanistan. The Mosque is said to be over 800 years old.

2017 – With US Army General (Four-Star) John William Nicholson, then-Commander of U.S. and NATO forces, Kabul, Afghanistan.

KABUL, Afghanistan (May 31, 2017) — General John Nicholson, Resolute Support commander, shakes hands with one of the first responders of the deadly attack that occurred here today. A vehicle-borne improvised explosive device was detonated near Zambaq Square outside the Green Zone, near diplomatic and government facilities. (U.S. Navy photo by Lt. j.g. Egdanis Torres Sierra, Resolute Support Public Affairs – Afghanistan)

2017 – Two certificates of appreciation by General Nicholson.

*2018 – Providing simultaneous (real time) interpretation
at a meeting of Strategic Communication (STRATCOM)
branches of the Afghan government and RSM at
Afghanistan's Government Media and Information Center
(GMIC), Kabul, Afghanistan.*

2019 – With Cornelius Zimmermann, NATO's Senior Civilian Representative/SCR (center); Mirwais Rahin, my boss at RSM's Linguistic Services Branch/LSB (center left); and my colleagues from LSB at the Headquarters of RSM, Kabul, Afghanistan.

2019 – With US Army Col. Patrick A. Disney, Director of Staff at RSM Headquarters, and my boss and colleagues from LSB, Kabul, Afghanistan. My recommendation letter to apply for the Special Immigration Visa (SIV) came from Col. Disney.

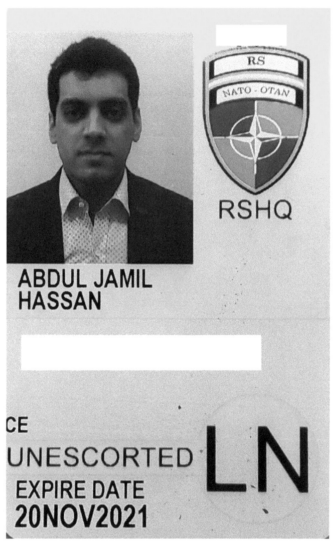

RS
NATO - OTAN

RSHQ

ABDUL JAMIL
HASSAN

CE
UNESCORTED LN
EXPIRE DATE
20NOV2021

2021 – My access badges; the yellow badge was for entering RSM's Headquarters and the blue badge was for access to CLASS II areas, where confidential documents and data were handled.

RESTRICTED

Division
DOS

Expires
14-FEB
2021

HASSAN
ABDUL JAMIL

Nationality
AFG

LCH-8

Geneva Conventions Identification Card

THE EVACUATION

Aug 18, 2021 – Waiting outside Kabul airport gate for the right time to get into the airport, Kabul, Afghanistan.

Aug 19, 2021 – With my family inside Kabul airport, right after crossing the airport gate, Kabul, Afghanistan.

Aug 20, 2021 – Under a US Air Force C-17 Cargo plane on the tarmac of US Air Force Base Al-Udeid, Doha, Qatar. The C-17 in the background was the plane my family and around 400 other Afghans flew in from Kabul.

Aug 21, 2021 – Inside a makeshift tent at US Air Force Base Ramstein, Germany.

Aug 2021 – The hangar and tents where we stayed for one week at US Air Force Base Ramstein, Germany.

Aug 2021 – Inside the hangar where my wife and daughter stayed for one week at US Air Force Base Ramstein, Germany. (My wife has taken the picture)

*Aug 23, 2021 - On the 2nd birthday of my daughter,
Lima, at US Air Force Base Ramstein, Germany.*

Aug 2021 – The hangar for in-processing and out-processing of evacuees at US Air Force Base Ramstein, Germany.

Aug 28, 2021 – With my family on board a United Airlines flight from US Air Force Base Ramstein (Germany) to the Dulles International Airport (USA).

Aug 31, 2021 – With my family at US Army Base Fort McCoy, Wisconsin, USA. We spent 65 days at Fort McCoy.

Sept 15, 2021 – My daughter, Lima, on the laps of Mr. Rahimi, one of our roommates at Fort McCoy. Lima and my father were so close to one another, and after fleeing Afghanistan, she thought Mr. Rahimi was her grandfather and would spend much time with him. Mr. Rahimi was also very kind to her.

Sept 2021 – Blocks designated for accommodation of Afghan evacuees at US Army Base Fort McCoy, Wisconsin, USA. We were accommodated in block #28.

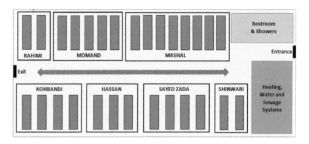

Sept 2021 – Layout of the room at US Army Base Fort McCoy, Wisconsin, USA. Seven families (28 people, women and children included) lived in the same room for over two months with no proper privacy at all.

Oct 2021 – Lines of Afghan evacuees outside one of the Dinning Facilities (DFACs) at US Army Base Fort McCoy, Wisconsin, USA. It took almost three hours for an individual to get one-time meal.

Oct 2021 – An example of meals provided to Afghan evacuees at US Army Base Fort McCoy, Wisconsin, USA. Quality and quantity of food were not good at all.

Oct 2021 – Providing voluntary linguistic services for agents of US Chamber of Commerce at US Army Base Fort McCoy, Wisconsin, USA. The agents provided crucial information twice a week to Afghan evacuees on employment opportunities across multiple industries in America.

Oct 01, 2021 – With US Army Captain Figeuroa, in-charge of two blocks of Afghan evacuees at US Army Fort McCoy, Wisconsin, USA. Captain Figeuroa was a true leader and spared no efforts in helping Afghan evacuees.

Nov 03, 2021 – Farewell with roommates – Hamid Mashal (first left), Nawid Kohbandi (second left), Hamza Mashal (first right) and Khalid Mashal (second right) – before leaving US Army Base Fort McCoy, Wisconsin for California.

Nov 21, 2021 – With my family near the Golden Gate Bridge in San Francisco, California, USA.

FAMILY LIFE & PERSONAL IMAGES

*1999 – With my oldest brother, Abdul Aziz, (left),
Herat, Afghanistan. We both worked at a store in a
food market before enrolling at a school in 2003.*

2012 – With my father and brothers during Eid
(Muslim Festival) days. It was the first time in
many years that all of us were at home for Eid.

2014 – With Parwiz Hazeq (center left), Barmal Akbari (center right) and my older brother, Abdul Habib Hassan (right), after casting votes during the presidential election, Kabul, Afghanistan. (Mr. Akbari is an SIV applicant but has been left behind in Afghanistan.)

2015 – At Azada Jirga (Open Discussion), a TV program jointly run by the BBC and RTA (Radio and Television of Afghanistan), Kabul, Afghanistan.

2016 – At a Model United Nations (MUN) conference, Kabul, Afghanistan. Delegates from around ten countries participated in the conference the purpose which was to learn how things are run at the UN.

2016 – With former Afghan President Ashraf Ghani at the Presidential Palace, Kabul, Afghanistan.

2016 – During an interview with a local TV in Bhubaneswar, the capital of India's Odisa state. I visited the country with thirty other Afghan students to attend an MUN conference.

2016 – Wearing traditional Afghan clothes, at India Gate,
a tourist site in the country's capital, New Delhi.

2018 – *Performing Atan, a traditional Afghan dance, at my own engagement party in Kabul, Afghanistan. Atan has been part of the Afghan culture for centuries.*

2020 – Judging at the final round of Afghanistan's Jessup International Law Moot Court Competitions, Kabul, Afghanistan, with Mr. Zarif Darkhili (left) and Mr. Shakeb Safi. In the back are the coach and members of the American University of Afghanistan (AUAF) who won the final round.

2021 – With my friends Firooz Farjam (center) and
Fraidoon Hakimi (right) in Herat, Afghanistan. I have
known them for over two decades, and they were the
ones who helped my family get included in the manifest
for evacuation by Italian forces.

*We're going to do everything — everything
that we can to provide safe evacuation
for our Afghan allies, partners, and Afghans
who might be targeted if — because of their
association with the United States.*

*We'll use every resource necessary to carry out
the mission at hand and bring to safety
American citizens and our Afghan allies.*

— President Joe Biden, August 2021

Last American Soldier leaves Afghanistan

Major General Chris Donahue, commander of the U.S. Army 82nd Airborne Division, XVIII Airborne Corps, boards a C-17 cargo plane at the Hamid Karzai International Airport in Kabul, Afghanistan. Maj. Gen. Donahue is the final American service member to depart Afghanistan; his departure closes the U.S. mission to evacuate American citizens, Afghan Special Immigrant Visa applicants, and vulnerable Afghans, August 30, 2021. (U.S. Army photo by Master Sgt. Alex Burnett)

For updated information,
news, and resources,
visit
PromisesBetrayed.com

About the Author

Abdul Jamil Hassan was born in 1986 in Zurmat District of Afghanistan's southeastern Paktia province. During the civil war his family moved to the capital, Kabul, and from there to Jalalabad City, the provincial capital of eastern Nangarhar province. A year after Taliban took control of Jalalabad, they migrated to Pakistan's Rawalpindi. In 1997, after a family friend assured their safety, they left Pakistan for Afghanistan's western Herat province where they spent 16 years. Jamil attended school, learned English and worked for over four years with Coalition Forces in Herat. In 2013, following his admission to Kabul University's Faculty of Law and Political Science, he lived, studied and worked in the Capital until he and his family escaped Afghanistan during the chaotic evacuation of August 2021.

Mr. Hassan has a degree in political science from Kabul University, and was supposed to defend the thesis for his Master's Degree in International Relations, a few days after August 15, 2021 when Taliban toppled the West-backed government of President Ashraf Ghani. Before serving with Coalition Forces (2008- 2012), Jamil worked as an ESL (English as Second Language) teacher in Herat. Following his graduation from Kabul University in 2017, he served as a high-level trilingual interpreter/translator at NATO's *Resolute Support Mission* headquarters in Afghanistan (RSMA) until a month before the events of August 15, 2021.

Jamil and his family arrived in Northern California in November, 2021, where they now live. He currently drives for Amazon, DoorDash and Uber Eats. He is now helping his wife learn how to drive. *Promises Betrayed* is the first book Mr. Hassan has ever written, and he considers it the most important achievement of his entire life so far.

ABOOKS

ALIVE Book Publishing
is an imprint of Advanced Publishing LLC,
3200 A Danville Blvd., Suite 204, Alamo, California 94507

Telephone: 925.837.7303
alivebookpublishing.com